# Computer Graphics and Animation:
# History, Careers, Expert Advice

Garth Gardner, Ph.D.

GARTH GARDNER COMPANY

*GGC publishing*

Washington DC, USA · London, UK

## Acknowledgment

I am indebted to the pioneers and practitioners who took the time to render their expert advice and account of historic events. Thanks also to my editor Bonney Ford, technical editor Jean Ippolito, art director Nic Banks, and the various individuals for their commitment to this project. A special thanks to my former professor Jane Veeder and road manager Terry Blum. Finally, thanks to the studios for opening their doors to me.

—GG

## About the Author

Garth Gardner, Ph.D. is a professor of animation and multimedia. He has taught and lectured at several universities including The Ohio State University, William Paterson University, University of California Los Angeles, Fashion Institute of Technology, Florida A&M University, University of Southern California, University of Texas at Austin, Xavier University, and George Mason University. He is a graduate of San Francisco State University and the Ohio State University.

## The Team

Editorial: Christina Gosnell, and Bonney Ford
Technical Editor: Jean Ippolito
Research Assistants: Dalia Gannam, Ryan Bell, Tomoko Miki, and Andrew Stubbs Johnston
Photographer: Lisa Lotti
Cover Image: Anton Gretchko

Editorial inquiries concerning this book should be e-mailed to: info@ggcinc.com. Website: www.gogardner.com

Library of Congress Cataloging-in-Publication Data

Gardner, Garth.
  Computer graphics and animation : history, careers, expert advice /
Garth Gardner.
      p. cm. — (Gardner's guide series)
Includes bibliographical references and index.
  ISBN 0-9661075-6-X
  1. Computer graphics. 2. Computer animation. 3. Computer
graphics—Vocational guidance. 4. Computer animation—Vocational
guidance. I. Title. II. Series.
T385 .G358 2002
006.6'023—dc21
                              2002008531

# Table of Contents

## Chapter 1

## Chapter 2

## Chapter 3

# Chapter 4

# Chapter 5

# Chapter 6

# Chapter 7

# Chapter 1
# Introduction

Proclaiming yourself a computer graphic artist has never been easier. Today, most people have access to an abundance of inexpensive computer equipment and graphics shareware via the Internet. In addition, there are several sites that cater to the beginning computer graphic artist. These sites offer free information and tutorials on the tricks of the computer art field, along with advice through interactive chat rooms. It is easy for one to look at this access to the latest software, even if it is on a trial basis and with inexpensive hardware. In the early days of computer graphics, scientists and artists fought for access to computers. Well, it is clear that for most of us that this struggle is over. Now we can finally begin to focus on the ART. But how does one become a computer graphics artist as a professional?

### The Seven Steps
The foundation of this book is based on seven recommended steps to becoming a computer graphics and animation artist:
1) **Study Traditional Fine Arts**
2) **Choose an Area of Concentration**
3) **Study the History and Theory of the Field**
4) **Learn the Tools of the Trade**
5) **Convey a Message With the Media**
6) **Prepare a Portfolio**
7) **Keep Current With the Changes in the Field**

### Step 1: Study Traditional Fine Arts

Learn to draw, paint, and develop an understanding of color. Computer art and animation is an art, and like other forms of art, it is important to understand the fundamentals of the field. Drawing is fundamental for all areas of computer graphics. To convey your ideas to a team, or to simply develop a storyboard for an animation, drawing skills are paramount. The study of fine arts practices will be important for an artist of new media to learn to conceptualize and to understand light, shape, form, and line. Studies in traditional fine arts for a prospective computer animator should also include the study of traditional animation. Learning hand-drawn animation and stop-motion, such as clay and paper manipulation is the proven method of understanding timing for animation. Animators should also study performance art such as dance, acting, and theatre.

## Step 2: Choose an Area of Concentration

The sooner you know what you want to do the better. While studying traditional fine arts fundamentals, you may also come across an area of traditional fine arts that you truly enjoy. Most areas of traditional fine arts can be channeled into an area of computer graphics. For example, creating fine arts sculpture is the fundamental for 3-D computer modeling; painting and color theory are fundamentals for texturing of a 3-D computer environment.

## Step 3: Study the History and Theory of the Field

Understanding the history is the key to true innovation in computer graphics and animation. The future growth of the computer graphics and animation fields will come about by the practitioners' understanding of past developments and trends. Beginners in this field should also have an understanding of the theories that govern good animation, such as Disney's principles of animation, and those borrowed from broadcast and filmmaking. This book does not address these theories. Suggested readings: *Sight, Sound, Motion: Applied Media Aesthetics* by Herbert Zettl and the *Disney Animation: The Illusion of Life* by Thomas Johnson and Ollie Johnson.

## Step 4: Learn the Tools of the Trade

This is a practical hands-on field and to produce results as an independent artist, one must learn the tools of the trade. This does not mean purchase a software package and learn how all the buttons work, but rather to explore several packages and understand the fundamentals of each. It often takes several software programs to create a single project. It is best to learn several packages and determine early, which works best for a particular project. Remember, there may be a number of software and hardware programs that work for any given project, but it is your duty to find the software that is most effective, efficient and best meets the demands of the project. Learn the popular program of the day, for example every artist of today should know Photoshop. In addition, 3-D animators should know 3-D packages such as Maya, Softimage, and 3-D Studio Max. Again, not cover to cover, but they should understand how and when to use these packages. If an artist is interested in compositing, for example, they should understand some of the hot compositing software out there today. Same goes for lighting, texture, modeling, etc.

**Step 5: Convey a Message With the Media**

You have the ability to take control of the medium. Convey a message that speaks of who you are as an artist, and your style and understanding of the aesthetics of the art. Do not become seduced by the slick capabilities of image processing software. The message is the framework of the story.

**Step 6: Prepare a Portfolio**

Creating a portfolio of your work or a demonstration reel of your animation is one of the most important steps in finding a job in the field or preparing for a gallery show. A portfolio should contain your best work, not necessarily your latest work. An animator's portfolio should include drawings, life drawings, studies of animals, clothed figures, and quick study sketches. A demo reel should express your understanding of timing. It is difficult to show timing using computer animation; however, a traditional animation section of your real can exhibit that skill. Timing can be shown best by using mediums such as claymation, cel animation, or stop-motion. Your portfolio should also show an understanding of perspective and composition. Color, lighting, and designing are all general requirements for any art portfolio. Be sure to have the job description in mind when assembling your portfolio. This visual field requires that prospective employees present examples of their art along with a resume. Educational credentials are often viewed as the steps necessary to achieve a great portfolio, not as a substitute for visual examples.

### Step 7: Keep Current With the Changes in the Field

"The computer is only a medium, and the medium should not be emphasized over the artistic results."
—A. Michael Noll

It's important to keep current with the technical and artistic changes in the field. This field is forever changing and it is important that its artists evolve with the field. Learning starts after school. Generally, the larger animation studios will train their new employees to use their proprietary software, and may later send them to receive training on particular commercial software. However, other small studios may not train; it then becomes the responsibility of the employee to learn the software. This is also true for aesthetics. Pixar University, for example, is an in-house training facility established to teach both technical and present art aesthetics. However, few other studios have such facilities. It is always the responsibility of the artist to keep current in the art of the field.

### Overview of Chapters

This book gives you a brief background of the history of computer graphics and answers a number of pressing questions often asked by beginners. While there is no one "right way" to becoming a computer graphic artist, this book will help guide you to a career in animation, multimedia, and visual effects.

This book incorporates information gathered through interviews with the pioneers and contemporaries of the field. In Chapter One, the book answers the most frequently asked questions of those entering the field in the 21st century. Information for getting started in the field of graphics is also discussed in this chapter. A section on defining computer graphics highlights some of the jargon used to define the many areas of this field. The first chapter also discusses the emergence of computer technology and digital effects as viewed in the context of traditional effects techniques.

Chapter 2, Areas of Specialty, describes some common careers in the field of computer art. Chapter 3 examines the history of the field from traditional effects techniques to computer graphics. Chapter 4 profiles selected pioneering fine artists and experimental computer animation artists. Chapter 5 takes a look at the history of digital visual effects as applied to the movie industry. Chapter 6 offers concrete advice to readers regarding training and education and universities versus self-training. Chapter 7 looks at your options for finding work as a computer graphics artist.

Arguably, being an artist in the computer graphics field is one of the most desirable career choices in the United States today. It is one of the few fields that allows art and computer technology to fuse in perfect harmony. Whether through fine arts or commercial visual effects, it is a field where improvements in the arts relate directly to the developments in the technology. In other words, the seemingly impossible becomes possible when the technology becomes available.

Perhaps few behind the scene professions are as enjoyable and rewarding as the visual effects artist profession. This field offers the artist the opportunity to create the unimaginable, making dreams a reality. Uniquely, this field is one that allows the artist to create and introduce to the world a character, object, or thing that was once merely a sketch and had never before been created. At the same time, the special effects field is complex, as it consists of various areas. The largest and most popular categories are traditional effects and digital effects. Though this book looks primarily at the artist who creates art through the use of computer graphics, fine arts, and commercial digital (visual) effects, it also explains the various traditional effects methods and the history of these two categories. In essence, commercial digital effects and computer graphics fine arts are not viewed as different provinces, but rather an attempt is made to show how they have learned from each other, whether the final objective is creating fine or commercial art.

It is still true that the most successful computer graphic projects rely on the creator's ability to combine fine arts with an understanding of the technology's capabilities. This is true for commercial and fine arts projects alike. Therefore, in discussing computer graphic art and commercial digital effects areas such as computer graphics, a discussion on the development of the tools and techniques of traditional effects cannot be neglected. In fact, discussion of how best to combine traditional and digital effects is a question of aesthetic and economics that is often investigated by the producers of effects projects. It requires a healthy combination of the two to create eye-catching results. Understanding both of these categories is essential for becoming a computer graphics artist.

### Is the Field Right For You?
When deciding whether computer graphics art is the best course of studies, you must first ask yourself if your are the right kind of person for the field. Do you enjoy working with computer technology? Are you a good communicator? Do you enjoy following directions? Do you like finding new solutions to familiar problems? Do you enjoy working with others as a team? If you answered yes to all these questions, then computer graphics may be the right path for you. Computer graphic production, like most other production fields, relies on teams of specialized individuals working towards a common goal often with impossible deadlines. And like most production fields, these specialized individuals work long hours to achieve the outcome of a completed assignment. However, unlike most production workers, most computer graphics practitioners are constantly intrigued by the ever-changing process and creating new solutions. Whether interactive games or film effects, few other production fields allow the practitioner the freedom to create anything imaginable, while receiving a generous income.

Working in the computer graphics field has its share of advantages and disadvantages. The following is a list of advantages and disadvantages associated with working in the computer graphics field.

## Advantages

Whether print-based graphic design or film effects, the commercial work usually receives national exposure.

Individuals working for a larger studio get to work on the latest hardware and software.

The artist can work on a wide variety of projects, often with the ability to experiment.

The team environment that is fostered by a computer graphics production can form lasting bonds among its workers.

Constantly changing software and hardware creates a continuous learning environment.

Computer processing time allows for frequent breaks in some areas of production.

Casual environment, no suits, no ties but still a white-collar environment.

## Disadvantages

Whether in a home-based studio or in a large production corporation, the computer graphics artist usually works long hours. A sixty- to eighty-hour work week is not unusual for feature film effects practitioners when in production.

Driven by management, deadlines are important and creative exploration may be limited.

The equipment for doing professional quality work is

costly, and must be updated often.

Limited creative licenses are given to junior artists and assistants.

The client is king and the artist must compromise with the client.

### Getting Started in the Computer Graphics Field

The computer graphics field is a large and complex field with many subdivisions. It is important to narrow your focus, and work toward a targeted goal. For example, are you interested in a career in computer animation, or a career in 3-D modeling? When selecting an area of emphasis within the computer graphics field, the first of many questions should be: Do you enjoy art or science? With most art-related fields, there is a science-related angle. For example, the science angle of fine arts painting may be chemically altering paint to create a desired color; knowledge of how much thinner to add to oil paint may be the closest to science that an oil painter may get. In the computer animation field, the scientist may be involved in the creation of the software or hardware that will in turn be used by the artist to create an animation. So, you can pursue an academic career in computer art or computer science and still gain employment in the computer graphics field. In fact, the computer scientist often works behind the scenes and is involved in the development of the mechanics and technology that enable the artist to create the art.

The second major division is with the choice of visual effects techniques. Are you interested in traditional effects or digital effects? The most common complaint beginning visual artists using the computer is the lack of tactile intuitive applications. A sculptor learning to use the computer to build 3-D models may discover that the computer is often slow to respond to this command; it is not intuitive or interactive in real-time. In fact, these issues may face anyone who is new to this medium; however, if this problem continues and the artist is not completely captivated by this digital medium there are still many other ways to pursue a visual effects career. 2-D computer graphics or traditional effects are just two of many other areas to explore. Although more and more traditional effects houses are beginning to incorporate more computer technology into their art, overall these traditional artists, such as stop-motion animators, still create with relatively little computer technology aid. They are able to build models by hand using techniques that rely on the animation of clay models and paper manipulation.

### Defining Terms

Over the last century, the terms used to describe the industry has been evolving. However, as the field grows and new terms are introduced, it appears that the old terms are still being used. This has become an issue that makes it difficult to use one word or phrase that encompasses the entire field. In this section, several terms are defined that will help you to understand the breadth of the field. This is the start of understanding some of the jargon in categorizing the areas of the industry.

In the late 1800s, film producers created avenues for incorporating visual effects in their productions. During this period, special effects techniques, such as the ones created in 1900 by a professional magician named George Méliès, fascinated theatre audiences. Méliès discovered that more than one image could be photographed on the same length of film. He astounded viewers by having people appear and disappear before their eyes with the first dissolve. His efforts to create illusionary films were simply referred to as tricks; however, these tricks were the exemplars used by many American film artists that followed. Today, these "tricks" are referred to as film effects.

As the film effects field continued to refine old techniques, a new province of effects was emerging. This was later known as digital effects. Far removed from the works of Méliès' early 1900s effects, the scientists of the mid 1900s began experiments with the computer that would later be called computer graphics. The computer would become an art tool and would be used by artists and scientists to create computer art.

With the advent of the computer as an art tool, a new

category of visual effects was created, and established terms were redefined. One resulting change in terminology caused by this paradigm shift is evident in the term "film effects." What was once called "film tricks" in the early 1900s is now called "traditional film effects." Computers complemented, and in some cases replaced, the need for traditional film effects. More importantly, it was another device used by the artist for creating art in addition to the many new tools created since the late 1800s. Unlike in the 1800s, when special effects were essentially a craft requiring a knowledge of clever carpentry and cabinet making in order to make ladies vanish and rabbits leap from a silk hat, the advent of the computer as an art tool meant an entirely new vocabulary.

A confusing variety of terms has been employed throughout the industry with reference to visual effects. The efforts of the visual effects artist was realized by the Academy of Motion Picture Arts and Sciences in 1963 when the Academy formally designated a separate award category for visual effects usually achieved in post-production. Before this time, optical effects were grouped together with mechanical and sound effects, under the general heading of special effects. Today, an overwhelming number of terms are used to describe special effects. Such terms as "visual effects" or "visual special effects" are used interchangeably to describe a general interdisciplinary art category of film effects. Since its introduction as a film effects tool, the computer has formed a contemporary branch of visual effects commonly referred to as digital effects, computer effects, and often computer-generated imagery. Traditionally, visual effects were called "optical effects cinematography." The terms "optical effects" or "optics" is synonymous with "special optical effects." The term "special visual effects" is used synonymously with "photographic effects" or simply "photo effects." Depending on the establishment, any of these terms are used with reference to the "optical effects cinematography." Today, however, optical effects, like digital effects, fall under the broad umbrella of film effects when used in the creation of shorts or feature-length films.

Broadly speaking, special effects work falls into two distinct categories: photographic effects (sometimes termed 'visual effects,' 'optical effects,' or 'process cinematography') and mechanical or physical effects. Photographic effects are as old as the motion picture itself. In fact, the principles that govern photographic effects were invented years before the advent of the motion picture. In the early days of motion picture, the cameraman himself (using only a camera and ingenuity) was responsible for a crude version of these effects. But it was the optical printer of the early 1930s, a single device that was able to produce the same effects and an astonishing number of others. Optical effects included such visual devices as fades, dissolves, superimposition, all the various matte work, rear projection, front projection, and so on. The term "visual effects" originally referred to the combination of the visual elements of two or more scenes into one single scene.

The visual effects industry comprises four specialized areas: storyboard, art directing, effects cinematography directing, and the effects production and animation. Optical effects are usually created by these departments through the use of special cameras, optical printers, animation, rotoscoping, or motion control. Optical effects can be as subtle as a red glow superimposed over a vampire's eyes or as spectacular as a dozen X-wing fighters attacking an imperial death star in outer space.

Max Fleisher created one of the earliest rotoscope devices in 1915. Rotoscope was used by Disney to aid in the production of Snow White and the Seven Dwarfs.

Stop-motion is a photographic visual effects technique that can be applied to both two-dimensional (2-D) and three-dimensional (3-D) environments. To achieve stop-motion, the artist splits up the motion of a film sequence into a series of still frames. Each still, which represents a frame of motion, is shot as a separate photograph in the motion sequence. The frames are then played on a film projector in sequence and the motion appears to be continuous. This technique of stop-motion is used in several methods of film animation, namely, claymation, paper manipulation, pixelation, and cel animation. In any of these methods, when the film is replayed at normal speed, the image photographed frame by frame, appears to move. This is due to a phenomenon of the human eye known as persistence of vision and it is proof that the camera not only can but does lie to us, with the collusion of our minds.

Mechanical effects are produced "live" in front of the camera. These effects are essentially a continuation of stage techniques—trap doors, wires, explosions, etc.—used for decades in live theatre. For example, mechanical devices were used to allow King Kong to grab an airplane out of the sky and to control a life-size model of a great white shark in Jaws. Mechanical effects can be defined as effects that incorporate the use of miniatures, or a puppet that, when operated mechanically, can simulate the motions of a creature, object, or human. This simulated motion can be either filmed simultaneously with the actors and actresses in the scene, or shot separately by a camera crew and combined with the other action in post-production. This technique of mechanical effects depends not only on skilled and innovative mechanics, but also on expert sculptors who can model convincing life forms, cast them into foam rubber and polyurethane forms, and finish them with colors and textures that will withstand the scrutiny of a close-up on a wide screen.

Photographic effects and mechanical effects make up the visual special effects industry. They are not often viewed as separate industries; instead, they complement each other. An example can be seen in stunt acts, which, when viewed independently, may be labeled mechanical effects, but the wires used to enable the stunt person to achieve these effects may be removed later through a technique known as "wire removal." Wire removal is a photographic effects technique that is commonly done today through the use of computer-generated imagery in post-production. The intent is to convey the thought, mood, and the imagination of the film writer or director. It is used as a seamless craft that blends fact and fiction and that may go unnoticed by the film audience.

Traditional visual effects were not produced to trick the public into believing that *King Kong* really existed or that a cybernetic organism was possible in the coming years; rather, they were economical means used to convince viewers of an illusion of reality on film. In definition, a special effect in a motion picture is any technique or device that is used to create an illusion of reality in a situation where it is not possible, economical, or safe to use the real thing. For example, in situations where it is not possible to make an object defy the laws of gravity and fly, the need to create the illusion of flight with visual effects is necessary. Special effects techniques have also made it possible to simulate natural conditions; rain or thunderstorms can be recreated through visual effects techniques. Matte painting has made it possible to transport a desert scene to a studio production through composite photography. It is not economical to build a complete set, if most of it can be done with a matte painting. It is not safe to have an actor jump through a plate-glass window, so harmless breaking resin is used. It is not reasonable to photograph your leading actor on a ledge forty stories above the street when the scene can be duplicated by trick photography on a studio set with absolute safety.

Mechanical effects techniques should not be confused with motion-controlled devices, which often aid visual special effects. A motion control system is an automatic camera system that usually consists of a mounted camera whose movement is electronically controlled. The camera is connected to a model stand, which stabilizes it and allows for vibration-free photography. The camera can be moved through a complete continuous or stop-motion shot. The exact repeatability of this lineage allows original-negative, multiple-exposure photography, with some shots lasting twelve to fourteen hours over several days. In some cases, the camera, automated in a model mount, is attached to motorized gimbals at the end of a long boom arm assembly. The boom, in turn, is usually attached to a motorized camera pedestal that rides on a precision track. The camera has eight axes of motion control to do in-camera streak, slit-scan, and single frame stop action cinema-

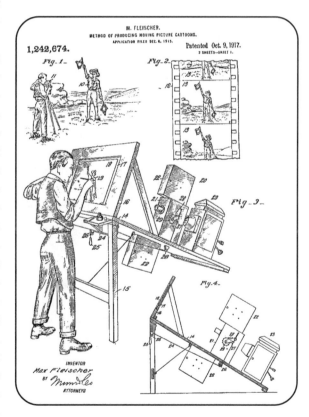

Max Fleisher, drawing of rotoscope devices 1915.

tography. Sometimes called electronic motion, this technique was used in the 1967 feature film, *2001: A Space Odyssey*, in which a computer-controlled electronic motion device was used to move a camera in seven different directions to allow special effects to repeat every move with perfect harmony. This device is neither a photographic nor mechanical effect; instead, it is a computerized mechanical tool that aids in the production of photographic effects.

Besides their use in the production of 3-D environments, traditional special effects are also used to produce 2-D characters and environments alike. Cel animation and paper manipulation are categorized as methods of 2-D effects that are produced through stop-motion techniques. Both methods of 2-D effects are produced solely through the use of photographic effects techniques; however, if combined with a 3-D environment, traditional effects may inherit the various qualities of mechanical effects or 3-D photographic effects, as in the case of *Who Framed Roger Rabbit*. In this feature film, both 2-D and 3-D effects techniques were combined. A process known as tone passes, produced through the use of the optical printer, was used to provide the 2-D animated cartoons with a roundness, which created a seamless blend between the 2-D characters and the live action actors.

Whether 2-D or 3-D, photographic or mechanical, visual effects techniques that precede digital effects are broadly referred to as having a conventional or traditional approach. These terms are used synonymously to describe and identify a style of visual effects that were done before the invention of digital effects, or effects that are done today but do not involve the use of computer graphics applications or programs. More specifically, the term "traditional special effects" is most commonly used in literature and various discourses to describe the general field.

Since 1950, computers have been incorporated into the arts. In 1967, computer graphics made its debut as a new form of visual effects used in the film industry. This new form of visual effects as a whole can be referred to as "contemporary effects." "Computer effects" or "digital effects" are terms used to describe specific areas of visual effects that are concerned mainly with the incorporation of computer-aided graphics when used in motion picture production. These effects are not limited to, but include morphing of live-action figures (the transformation or computer interpolation from a 2-D or 3-D computer data to another image data over a defined number of frames), modeling of 3-D environments (building or displaying 3-D computer data), textural mapping (2-D digital information used to form the surface quality of a 3-D computer image data), and many others.

*Geri's Game* created at Pixar Animation Studio is an example of high-end 3D computer models. Image courtesy Pixar Animation Studios

As more computer effects artists attempt to simulate the techniques and tools of the traditional effects artists, and as more traditional effects artists learn more about the computer, the gap between traditional and contemporary effects techniques will narrow. This will cause some terms used to describe traditional and contemporary effects techniques to become acceptable and interchangeable and may cause others to become obsolete.

Traditional effects artists may specialize in stop-motion animation, claymation, or mechanical effects. The computer graphics (CG) artist may focus on animation, fine arts, modeling, multimedia, or digital video.

# Chapter 2
# Computer Animation
# & Graphics

Areas of Specialty

When a large studio such as PDI/DreamWorks or Pixar creates a feature 3-D animation, several steps must be taken. The steps taken at the larger studios are similar to those taken at a small studio that may be working on a 30-second TV commercial. The main differences are the extra steps necessary for introducing the project to the client and selling the idea to them in the pitch. Large commercial studios take the following steps in creating a 3-D feature animation. These steps are often referred to as the animation pipeline.

| PRE-Production |
| --- |
| Script |
| Pitch |
| Storyboard |
| Recording |
| Animatic |
| Design |

| Production |
| --- |
| Modeling |
| Layout |
| Set Dressing |
| Animation |
| Texture |
| Lighting |

| POST-Production |
| --- |
| Rendering |
| Compositing |
| Editing |
| Sound fx |

1) **Pitching** the animation story idea to a client. Some studios are their own client and may create a movie and have it distributed outside, while other studios create movies for outside clients. In either case, the idea must be sold to get funding. A sales pitch must be developed. An animation script may accompany this pitch.

2) The artist transforms the animation script into drawings called a **storyboard**. The storyboard is a series of drawings that maps out the story and characters in boxes called panels. A text box for dialogue is normally included. The studio's art department draws the storyboard.

3) Recording of the **voices**. After the idea gets the green light for funding, human voices (voice actors) are recorded for the characters.

4) The next step is the **storyboard animatic**, which marries the voices from the storyboard to videotape. An animatic is a movie of storyboard stills, which includes recorded voice dialogue. It is the layout of the various scenes in the animation in sequence.

5) The **Art Department** finalizes the look and feel of the charac-

ters on a character sheet. This stipulates the official look for the characters.

6) Next, **models** are built on the computer—and sometimes without the computer—in the form of sculptural models. Sculptural models are scanned into the computer through the use of 3-D scanning devices.

7) **Layout** of the various shots using the 3-D computer models is next. The models are positioned to stage the key parts of the scenes in this step.

8) **Set designing** is necessary to determine the color and textural element for the objects in the characters' environment. This is often referred to as set dressing.

9) **Animation** of the models on the computer using 3-D animation software is the next step in the process.

10) Applying **shaders** to the characters and environment to determine color and **texture,** whether cloth, wood grain, or wallpaper is necessary.

11) Digital **lighting** of the scenes to establish time of day, mood, and environment is also an important step in animation.

12) **Rendering** and compositing gives the computer animation its final look. The scenes are rendered and the images are composited or superimposed to create one image. Compositing is used when the scene calls for live action to be layered with computer animation or for speeding up the rendering process in a fully computer animated movie.

13) **Post-production** effects are added for drama, such as environmental sound, dramatic sound effects, and musical scores. This is also the stage where different rendered segments may be composited. This department also edits the film under the watchful eye of the director.

Careers

This flow chart merely provides a template for a basic flow of a 3-D computer animation production. Whether commercial or experimental, computer graphics and animation is achieved through an interdisciplinary process. This process includes a mix of writing, art, design, science, and often sound to make possible the extraordinary effects we see in our everyday lives. Each specialty area borrows from the other and no area is totally independent of the others. The areas of specialty are also careers within the computer graphics and animation industry. In this section, we will explore and define some of the most common careers for artists and designers in the graphics and animation industry.

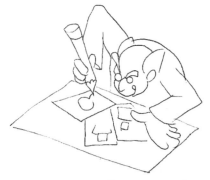

### Concept and Story

The first stage in design or art is having a concept. In the commercial world, this is often assigned by a client or advertising agency. The artist and designer must then begin the process of bringing that concept to fruition. In the commercial environment, an illustrator at the company's graphic design department usually sketches the concept out. The illustrator at an animation company, for example, works directly with the director to interpret the script, in a series of drawings that represents the key action in the various scenes. These drawings, a little larger than a thumbnail sketch, are assembled on a board in the order of events. This board is called a storyboard. It includes a text box at the bottom of the key frames that provides information about the action within the scene and directional arrows that are used to direct the camera's movement. The storyboard is one of the first stages of visually representing the

*Sleepy Guy*, storyboard segment courtesy Pacific Data Image

scenes of an animation, video, or any form of moving graphics. The number of drawings needed depends on the number of scenes within the story. Over 4,000 storyboard drawings (panels) were created for the action and dialogue for Pixar's feature-length animation, *Toy Story*.

In the design of still graphics, a concept drawing may be the most appropriate. The concept sketch is the designer's method for visualizing the rudiments of the design with the art director. Similar sketches, often done in full color, are used in the designing of characters of an animation. They are then called character studies. What is the character going to look like? How can it be given appeal? These are the questions considered before the drawing is passed on to the concept artist to determine the final polished look.

The character designer, storyboard artist, and designers in this stage of production are merely proposing various ideas for the director. When the director accepts the rough concepts, the concept artist then finalizes the work, with fully-rendered color. This work is then presented to the client for approval. The concept drawings are usually revised during the creative-development process.

### Modeling

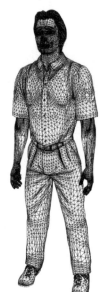

Crewman Model courtesy ViewPoint DataLab, Int'l., Inc.

Modeling also has its share of off-the-computer planning. Often, before the model is built, a marquette (a physical miniature model) is done to determine the actual form of the character. Modeling is the term used to describe the building of a 3-D object or model. Models are built through the use of nurbs-based or polygon-based geometry. There are several different ways to build a model on the computer. A basic model is constructed by grouping primitives, such as a sphere, cylinder, cube, or cone together to form an object or single geometry. A more complex model may be derived through joining various patch surfaces together or by pushing and pulling the curve vertices of a primitive to form an object. This method is known as procedural modeling and can be done explicitly, where the modeler actually interacts with the model

and molds the shape in a similar fashion to that of a sculptor molding clay; and it can be done implicitly by imputing codes into the computer that affects the shape of the object. A model may also start with a curve profile that is then rotated to form a bottle, glass, or other round symmetrical object.

At Rhythm and Hues, modeling manager Keith Hunter created a 3-D animation short called *Prime Ordeal*; a piece he had been working on for five years prior to its release in 1998. The model was constructed from polygons and the background model *Prime-Ordeal* is comprised of 65,000 polygons. The design for the complex character began from a sketch Hunter made on paper. At Rhythm and Hues, he primarily used proprietary modeling software to create the models.

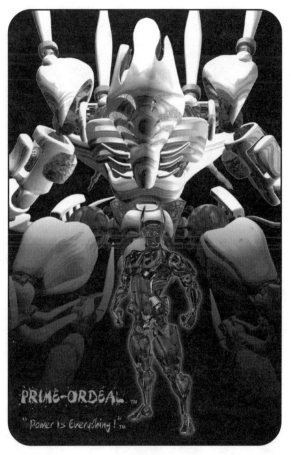

Models from Prime-Ordeal created by Keith Hunter

Top Left: *Alien Resurrection*, computer model courtesy Twentieth Century Fox

## Animation

Animation can fall into two general categories: traditional animation and computer animation. Traditional animation can be defined as animation that is created through the use of photographic film techniques. More specifically, traditional animation is comprised of the following styles: claymation, pixelation, cel animation, paper manipulation, and stop-motion. One of the most popular styles of ani-

Cel animators inbetweeners and stop-motion animator all at Curious Pictures, NY.

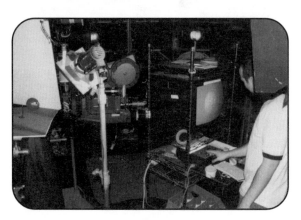

mation is cel animation. Cel animation began circa 1915 when animation pioneers John Bray and Earl Hurd created and patented the technique called celluloid animation. This technique would become the standard technique used in the creation of hand-drawn animation. The cel, as it was called, allowed the artist to create layered imagery; thus allowing the animator to animate portions of a scene without redrawing the entire scene. Instead, the animator only redrew the parts of the image that were being animated. Walt Disney popularized this technique of classical animation. The *Lion King* and *The Little Mermaid* are examples of cel animation used today.

The technique of stop-motion is generally applicable to all traditional 3-D models that are animated. The technique of stop-motion makes it possible to animate most objects whether inanimate or animate. The stop-motion technique can be used to make a clay figure come to life; this is known as claymation. To create the illusion that a human being is moving in an irregular fashion, a stop-motion technique called pixelation is used. Pixelation uses a live action cast and traditional stop-motion film techniques to create an animation. Stop-motion is achieved when the animator manually moves each frame and shoots a picture in a consecutive series of stills, which when played back creates the illusion of motion. In theory, the illusion of smoothness exists because of a plurality in the human-vision system. The mind will retain a single picture for a brief period of time. If a series of closely related pictures are shown quickly in order, the new picture will arrive before the old one fades. The se-

ries of pictures are then perceived as a smooth movement. This theory is known as persistence of vision. If
the difference between successive pictures are too large
or the time between them is too long, then the illusion
is shattered and the motion no longer appears smooth.
Research has shown that with film, 24 consecutive
frames-per-second and in video 30 frames-per-second
achieves successful persistence of vision with humans.

On the production of Weird Al's music
video *Jurassic Park.* Courtesy Scotti Bros.
Records. Photo credit: Lester Cohen

Traditional animation must be created frame-
by-frame whereby the animator must calculate each frame and
adjust for timing throughout the animation. The traditional animator usually shoots the work directly to film and is unable to see
the results of the motion until the film is developed. This animator
must shoot 24 frames for every 1 second of animation when using
16 millimeter film. Therefore, in creating a 90-minute film, the
traditional animator must create 24 frames times 60 seconds times
90 minutes equal to 64,800 frames per feature film.

The traditional anima-
tion industry is made up of various specialists, and the animation is usually done by a team
of practitioners. On a cel animation project, these teams may
be comprised of animators,
inbetweeners, character designers, storyboard artists, colorists,
background scene painters,
inkers, creative directors, etc. A
stop-motion animation team
differs from a cel animation
team as they create 3-D models
that can be animated. The stop-

*Harvest,* a 3D computer animation
courtesy Xaos, Inc.

motion animation team may be comprised of storyboard artists,
character developers, modelers, animators, creative directors, etc.

Whether produced on a high-end or low-end workstation
using proprietary or turnkey software, computer animation is simply animation created on the computer. Computer animation is

*Gas Planet,* courtesy Pacific Data Image. This 3-D computer animation has the appearance of a traditional cel animation

usually referred to as high-end or low-end. The difference relies on the type of workstation more than the type of software used to create the animation. Animation that is created on the Sun, Silicon Graphics, and NT workstations are typically referred to as high-end animation. Animation created on the Macintosh, Amiga, and personal computers are typically referred to as low-end animation. High-end animation are the ones we typically see in feature films. Films such as *Toy Story* and *Jurassic Park* show the level of complexity that is attainable only on high-end workstations through the use of turnkey and proprietary software. Proprietary software is that which is written by an individual for a specific project or studio but not available commercially. Commercially available software is referred to as turnkey or off-the-shelf software. Today, proprietary software is often used along with turnkey software.

Computer animation consists of two divisions: two-dimensional (2-D) and three-dimensional (3-D) animation. Also referred to as computer graphic imagery (CGI), computer animation is a compilation of still computer graphic images. 2-D computer animation is created through the use of 2-D animation software programs that allow the artist to draw a series of images on the computer and play it back as animation. This method of animation can be compared to traditional cel animation or paper manipulation, as 2-D computer animation can also be created through

*Wet Waltz* a 3-D animation by Xaos, Inc. The animation used motion capture techniques to create liquid humanlike animated figure.

the use of digitized or scanned images. The computer allows the 2-D computer animator the immediate gratification of reviewing the animation at any stage of production. The 2-D computer animator can also make changes in color and add or delete frames to perfect the animation.

3-D computer animation can be compared to traditional

claymation as it requires similar steps in the stages of production. First, a model must be built before the animation can take place. In the computer environment, this means the construction of a wire-frame model through the use of a 3-D modeling or animation package. Depending on the model, a skeleton must be built. Like an armature on a claymation character, skeletons are usually created for models such as a figure that requires complex motion throughout the animation. Similar to a clay character's armature, in a digital environment the skeletons are grouped to the model. This allows the 3-D model to be key-framed by establishing the skeleton's key position. After the model and the necessary skeletons are made, the 3-D animator may move to the stage of creating textures or shaders for the model. These textures and shaders are applied to the object to represent the final color and texture of the models. The 3-D animator must also assign digital lights to the model's environment. The animation is normally roughed out through a technique known as a

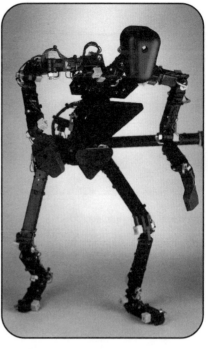

blocking. Blocking is used by the animator to explore the timing and to work out issues in the animation by substituting the finished model with primitives such as cubes and spheres. These primitives are temporarily grouped to the final skeleton. This technique allows the animator to visualize and choreograph the motion before applying the geometry intensive final model. After the motion is finalized, the textures are selected and the lighting set, the animation is rendered as the final animation and output to tape. The

The Monkey2 digital input device shown above courtesy Digital Image Design Inc. is a performance capture system used by 3-D animators.

MotionStar Wireless system (left), image courtesy Ascension Technology Corporation. This motion capture system is used to input a human's motion into the computer. The information inputted is then applied to 3D computer model to create an animation. This system is often used to speed up the animation process, or to create more precise human motion.

Traditional animation studio at Curious Pictures, NY.

complex stages of producing a 3-D animation has created a number of specialized areas such as modeling, technical directing, creative directing, lighting and texture specialization.

Integration of computer graphics with traditional animation has become more prevalent in the industry today. At many traditional cel animation companies, 2-D computer paint programs are now used to create traditional animation cel and background painting. That is because the computer has become an economically viable alternative when compared to the painstaking task of painting cels by hand. In most cases, the use of cels has been eliminated altogether, replaced by a computer attached to a high-tech scanner that is used to input the drawings into a software program. The traditional background painter who once painted realistic scenes with a paintbrush and airbrush has been introduced to the concept of painting with light. Nearly all forms of traditional animation from claymation to paper manipulation to cel animation have integrated computer technology and its graphics to simplify, economize, or to simply improve the aesthetics and overall appeal. Traditional animators may be turning to computer graphics to enhance their production in the same way that computer graphics animators turn to traditional animation. Computer animators often study the Disney principles of traditional animation and apply these principles to computer animation and the aesthetics. Unsatisfied with the early computer animation productions, today most computer animators may study the works of legendary traditional animators to aid them in addressing concerns of aesthetics and to gain a better understanding of motion. Whether traditional or computer, the definition of animation remains the same: a motion picture made by the assemblage of a series of progressive still images that simulates motion.

It is important to note that the computer animation profession is divided into two distinct categories: commercial animation and experimental animation. So far we have discussed the various ways in which animation can be created through the use of traditional methods, such as stop-motion animation or conventional methods such as computer animation. Whether an artist animates for pay or for personal pleasure is the basis of these two new categories.

Commercial animation art is often produced by an animation firm or an independent animator contracted by an advertising agency. As the name implies, the goal of a commercial animation is to advertise products, goods, or services. Commercial animators are also employed to work on feature films for scenes that require animation or digital special effects. The commercial animator often works from a storyboard and is usually supervised by an art director from the advertising agency. In some cases, the commercial animator may propose a storyboarded concept directly to a corporation. This allows the commercial animation firm more flexibility to direct the commercial. After a storyboard is agreed upon, the animation company will have it signed off by the client. This written acknowledgment of the storyboard is important for determining the cost and duration of production.

The experimental animator is usually an independent animator that is creating for the sole purpose of expression. The animation may range from narrative to abstractly conceptual. There are usually no absolute deadlines and no tightly scripted storyboards. The only limitation for the artist may be access to high-end equipment although that is not necessary to create their animation, because the experimental animator is resourceful and uses whatever is available. The goal, for artists of this caliber, is usually to show their creative work at animation festivals, galleries, and museums to gather attention for themselves and their ideas. They may receive grants and endowments to fund the productions done at their studios. Other experimental animators may gain access to equipment through universities that support their research or through large technological corporations such as Bell Labs for use in research.

## Shading and Lighting Artist
In the area of 3-D computer animation, the animators neither draw the animated frames, or ink or paint the scenes as is required in

traditional animation. Instead, digital methods are employed to give the 3-D geometry its final polished look. The department of lighting and texture take over the process after the animators have completed the final motion of the geometry. First, shaders are applied to the wire-frame geometry. Shaders are computer programs that describe surface characteristics, including textures, bumps, and finishes for every object in the scene. These programs can simulate any attribute, such as wood, metal, cloth, and most any imaginable surface. Practitioners in the shading area are mainly concerned with the replication of the material to create the ideal look for the animation. They may often find real objects and materials that can be scanned into the computer and stored as texture maps. The scanned image can then be assigned to geometry through a procedure called texture mapping. The texture is then locked to the surface of the geometry and moves with the object.

In the lighting stage, the characters and scenes are lit; this process employs the use of digital lights on the computer. Much like traditional stage lighting for live-action film, the digital light parameters such as hue, saturation, and color can be adjusted. In the case of digital lights, the practitioner can change these parameters with little effort. For example, instead of adding gels to change the colors of lights as is the practice in a traditional environment, the digital lighter can merely change the values of the light's color to result in a change by pushing a button on a keyboard. As traditional film, lights are used to enhance the mood and emotion of the scenes.

*Bingo* an animation by Chris Landreth.

The 3-D computer animation is given its final look in the rendering stage. This process requires the computer, through the use of rendering software, to calculate such things as color, texture, and form. The renderer determines the attributes and parameters for the object and its 3-D environment.

## Computer Art

Computer art, computer imagery, electronic art, digital art, and any other terms used to describe fine arts created on the computer can be referred to as a fusion of art and computer technology.

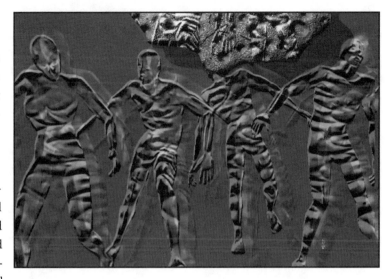

*Impressions,* computer Imagery by author.

Computer art, as it is most commonly referred to as, can be commercial-based or fine arts-based. In the case of a commercial artist creating work as part of a computer graphic production, it is commonly referred to as digital art. These digital artists usually have a fine arts background and a good sense of color and painting aesthetics. They are often employed in the area of digital matte painting or as lighting and texture specialists.

The computer is one of the latest devices to be integrated into the fine arts arena, both as a tool and as a medium. The computer may be viewed as a tool since it is used by the artist to create the art, and as a medium since it is often used to display the art. With the computer comes a new generation of artists eager to explore its potential as a fine arts medium. Fine artists may seek to exhibit their works in a museum or gallery. The works of computer artists may vary from large format prints to 3-D sculptural art to computer experimental animation. Computer artists have been able to integrate the computer technology into all forms of traditional fine arts. The areas of specialization are endless. A computer fine artist can be involved in a number of creative mediums and mixed mediums and techniques, such as applying traditional paint over a computer print. Or they can be involved in a

*Jabio* a digitally altered photo created by Joel Slayton

3D computer fine art Image courtesy
Charles Csuri

"Living in 1984, the role of the artist has to be different from what it was fifty or even twenty years ago. I am continually amazed at the number of artists who continue to work as if the camera were never invented, as if Andy Warhol never existed, as if airplanes, and computers, and videotape were never heard of."
— Andy Warhol, 1984

single medium—the computer. Computer fine artists can create and display their art within the confines of the computer. For example, interactive art. This art form is usually not printed and remains within the computer and is displayed on the monitor. On the other hand, some fine artists prefer working toward a more traditional art object. Their work is output through a printer to film, fabric, wood, and any other material imaginable. Like traditional fine artists, they often begin by sketching out the concept on paper and, in the case of 2-D based computer art, they may then draw directly on the computer or scan in images and perform a number of functions, often referred to as image processing. They may incorporate different scanned photos and end their work as a digital collage, or they may work from one image that is processed. Computer fine arts can also be created entirely from 3-D built models and objects with expressive textures.

Whether digital art or computer fine arts, the two must find a venue to exhibit their work. The digital artists at the commercial environment of a computer graphics production company have the opportunity to see their work incorporated into TV commercials or feature films along with the contribution of the entire production staff. Since they work for a company, commercial artists receive a salary but their art then belongs to the client or the production house. The computer fine artist usually exhibits his/her work at a gallery and in print-based media. Unless commissioned to create a work of art, the computer fine artist usually owns the work created and is free to price and sell the work of art.

### Interactive/Multimedia

Interactive refers to software or hardware that is designed to facilitate human interaction. A basic example of an interactive device is the computer keyboard—this device is created solely for the purpose of human interaction. Of course today the word *interactive* may overlook such basic examples as the touch screen, since this allows for interaction with an image on screen. Multimedia is used to describe a technology-based project that uses various devices to create one work, as in a multimedia workstation. A single multimedia project may employ the use of various areas such as video, computer graphics, and high-end animation. Another multimedia project may simply be comprised of a video deck that is accessed through a single computer program that allows the viewer to access various parts of the video by clicking on different interactive buttons using the mouse or keyboard. Like most of the computer graphics areas, multimedia can also be divided into high-end and low-end. It may be used to solve a specific commercial problem, such as a touch screen that allows a mall shopper to view different parts of the mall through video or more experimental as in the case of a fine arts installation. There is no clear distinction between high-end and low-end interactive multimedia. Unlike high-end animation, a high-end interactive multimedia project relies less on the level of the operating system and more on the artist's ability to program, design, and create on any given platform. A high-end interactive multimedia project can be created on a low-end workstation.

## Visual Effects

Referred to as special effects, this area of specialty has the task of putting anything imaginable on screen. If the film script calls for a bullet hit or a bombing of an entire city, it is all within a day's work for the film effects department. With a goal to enhance communication by visual means, the film effects artist creates effects through the use of optical, physical, or digital effects techniques. The film effects artist's only limitation may be the budget; so, the larger the effects budget, the more technically sophisticated the effects will be. However, even in the early days of trick effects, the effects director knew that you could get away with marginal effects once the audience was caught up in the story. Today, this is still true. Even with the increasing budgets for film effects, the feature film's commercial success hinges on the story even more than its effects.

## Multimedia Team Structure

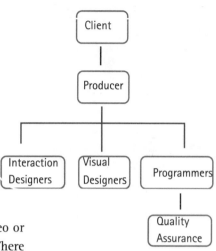

The above chart offers the basic structure followed by multimedia studios, such as video game design studios. Below the design studio may follow these step in completing the project for client. The broad design decisions are made at the top. Each stage ends with the client's approval. Diagrams courtesy Chris Swain.

## Development Process

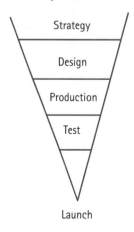

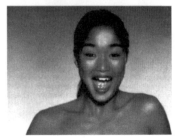

Courtesy MJ Productions, Morphing by PDI

## Virtual Reality (VR)

As a specialty area, virtual reality (VR) encompasses various areas of computer graphics, including computer programming, modeling, animation, texturing, lighting, and rendering. VR is primarily used today in the entertainment and medical field. If you have been to a video game arcade recently, you probably noticed that most of the games included some form of interactivity. Whether you are shooting at a computer-generated figure or racing around a track in the automobile racing games, you are interacting in a virtual world—a world created on the computer that often includes characters programmed to react to your choices. This is a basic form of virtual reality. In fact, if you were to reduce these gaming screens to two small screens about 2" square to maintain stereo vision, and set them 4" from the pupils of your eyes, and fit them into wearable goggles that block off any lights from the natural environment, the same game virtual world would become a simulated reality. It then becomes true VR when the participant can see a real-time computer simulation of themselves from their point of view, usually interacting with other virtual objects.

## Design

The computer has become the tool of choice for various forms of traditional designers. Such traditional areas as graphic design, industrial, and product design now incorporate the computer as one of the chief design tools. The computer has also impacted traditional design practices. For example, illustration has facilitated a new area called Web design. Web design has become a major area of interest for young graphic designers to express their designs beyond the print medium.

The areas of industrial design and product and interior design have traditionally relied on hand-built models to aid in the visualization of the final product. This is still true today, but with a few changes. Models are now built on the computer using various Computer Aided Design (CAD) and computer animation software programs. These computer technologies not only allow the designer to build more representational models, but also allow for economical alteration at the client's request. Small industrial design firms may contract a data lab to create the models to their specifications, whereas, larger firms may create the data model in-house. For example, an interior design firm may use digitally created models of interiors and may choose to present them to the client via a 3-D animation program or through an interactive program that allows for client participation.

Graphic design is perhaps one of the most diverse computer graphics areas. It can be viewed as an umbrella that encompasses specialized areas such as web design and interface design. Graphic design consists of two major categories: print-based and media-based graphics. Common to these areas is the computer. Whether the design is printed to paper as the final output or displayed on the computer or video display monitor, it is media-based. The computer is the primary tool used today to create graphic design.

## Conclusion

The final computer graphic image is a result of a well planned out process for constructing the image. There are many different areas of specialization in the field of computer graphics described in this chapter. The areas mentioned here are some of the main career options within the field of computer graphics. Of the areas described, concept and story are at the forefront of all computer graphics. At this stage the storyboards or flow charts are created to instill accuracy in communicating the concept or idea. Modeling is limited to 3-D computer graphics images and individuals in this area are responsible for building of the objects or models on the computer. The 3-D models are given life in the animation area.

*Knick Knack* courtesy Pixar Animation Studios. A still image from the 3D animated short film

However, animation is not limited to 3-D computer graphics. It consists of 2-D, hand-drawn figures and 3-D, stop-motion characters done through the use of traditional animation. Shaders, lighting, and textures are technical areas whereby the images are given the final look. Within a 3-D scene, the final hues and image are rendered on the computer. Lighting and texture is limited to 3-D computer graphics. More general terms such as computer art are used to describe an area of specialization where the computer is used to create fine arts images. Interactive/multimedia practitioners are involved with using various digital mediums creating an environment; they program the computer to respond to commands inputted by a human. The computer is often at the center of the multimedia device and acts as the programmable brain, the central processing unit. Virtual reality has become an interactive multimedia area, encompassing various areas of computer graphics including modeling, animation, shaders, lighting, textures, and rendering, in addition to software engineering and programming. Design is another major area that uses computer graphics. Such as graphics design, interior design, and Computer Aided Design (CAD) are some of the main areas for design.

# Chapter 3
# Traditional Animation Techniques

## A Brief History

### Antecedents

The intellectual heritage behind the theory of visual effects as used by artists over the years is complex and wide-ranging. Unfortunately, the origins of visual effects are not well-known, and most literature has neglected to mention the names of many of the artists and scientists who contributed to its birth (Spellerberg, 1980). In this chapter, I will highlight some of the artists and scientists who were pioneers in the early art and technology used to create visual effects. This is an important step in beginning to show the complexity of this field that seemingly started trick effects, and whose focuses continues to shift in techniques from trick effects to stop-motion, animated drawings to go-motion, to visual effects. The techniques discussed in this chapter are all traditional and does not involve the use of computer technology. These traditional developments were the basis for computer graphics and high-end animation.

### Pre-Film: Development of Traditional Visual Effects

Visual effects involve both art and science. Its artistic roots can be traced to the court magician, who created wondrous illusions to astound and entertain. Its scientific aspect was developed by engineers with a good understanding of practical physics (Hutchison 1987). However, it is my belief that scientists and artists drive each other's creativity; this is seen throughout the history of visual effects. Early audiences were less demanding and just the novelty of movement was sufficient to provide entertainment. As the equipment techniques and audience became more sophisticated, it was important for the arts to incorporate technology to create more elaborate effects to keep the audience's interest.

Fry and Fourson (1977) write, "The story of motion pictures starts with when Aristotle developed the basic theory of optics; Archimedes began experiments with lens and mirrors, and an Arab named Alhazen pioneered the study of the human eye" (p. 5). A German priest and mathematics professor named Athanusius Kircher has been credited with the invention of the first crude slide projector in 1644. As a result of his numerous impressive inventions, Kircher earned the title of "Doctor of a Hundred Arts" (Fry and Fourzon 1977). This begins our historic timeline.

1602    Athanusius Kircher was born in Germany.

1646    Kircher's work with magic lanterns, projections, and his observations on the major shadow art-science was related in his book, *The Great Art of Light and Shadow*, published in Rome. The first nine chapters of his book included such diverse topics as "light, reflection, images, the speaking tube, the structure of the eye, sketching devices, the art of painting, geometrical patterns, clocks, the nature of reflected light, refraction and means of measuring the earth" (Quigley, Jr. 1948 p.52). The tenth section of his book is divided into three sections where he discusses the story of Magic Shadow and explains the use of mirrors and reflections. This section also detailed the various types of mirrors such as convex, concave, and spherical. He was viewed by the public as being in a league with the devil on account of his power with mirrors, lenses, and amazing projected images; nevertheless, Kircher's name as "The Doctor of a Hundred Arts" spread throughout the European world. People began to understand and appreciate his magic projection through the use of mirrors. In the months following its announcement, the magic lantern was distributed widely by vagabonds and impostors, all claiming it as their own invention.

1658    Apart from Kircher himself, four other men made the magic lantern projector principle and construction widely known. These men were Gaspar Schott, Claude Milliet de Chales, Johann Zahn, and William Molyneux. Gaspar Schott, a protégé of Kircher, was known for his book, *Wonders of Universal Nature and Art,* published in 1658, with a second edition in 1674.

1680    Kircher died. By this time, his lantern was widely used in Europe for scientific and entertainment purposes, as in the art of deception. His Magic lantern allowed magicians to become the kings of entertainment between the middle of the seventeenth century to the late nineteenth century and beyond. Special magic theatres and grand tours were popular arenas for family entertainment. Evidence has also shown that the original design of the lantern was used by magicians up to the late nineteenth century.

1690    As a showman, Zahn demonstrated how images could be projected under water. William Molyneux, a proclaimed scientist and teacher, further developed the lantern by adding focusing lenses. The lantern served as an entertainment and magician's tool for creating visual effects. "By the early part of the eighteenth century, the magic lantern was commonplace and men were skilled in its use" (Quigley, Jr. 1969 p. 69).

1845    A French magician, Jean Eugene Robert-Houdin, "the father of modern magic," founded a theatre in Paris that produced magic shows for more than seventy years. The theatre workshops produced a continual series of new illusions, including optical effects using multiple magic lanterns. The optical creations became an especially important part of Theatre Robert-Houdin in 1888, when the theatre was owned and managed by George Méliès (Barnouw 1981).

## Pre-Computer: Development of Visual Effects in Film

Brosnan (1974) writes,

The beginning of the story of special effects is to be found at the beginning of the film industry itself. Not long after the first image had been successfully projected onto a screen, trick photography, the creating of illusions through the manipulation of camera and film, was born. But one of the most exasperating things about any investigation into the development of the film industry is the difficulty of attempting to determine just who was first with any particular technique or device. This is because so many of the early pioneers were working independently, separated by both natural boundaries and business competition... it is more or less impossible to state with any certainty just who invented trick photography, but we can at least group together those who were among the first...(p.15)

Thomas Edison and his assistant William Dickson together applied Kircher's theories of optics. The two began working on these problems in 1887. Shortly after, they discovered that film was the way to reproduce moving images. Although Edison and his assistant had the right concept for reproducing moving images, they were unable to develop the right photographic emulsion to make it work. The problem Edison faced was similar to that of George Eastman, who around the same time was working on the production of a simple snapshot camera for the amateur photographer.

Eastman, completely absorbed in photography, sought to simplify the complicated process of producing an image. He began reading British magazines in which photographers were publishing their findings upon making their own gelatin emulsions. Using a formula taken from one of these British journals, Eastman began making gelatin emulsions. This concept led to three years of photographic experiments by Eastman. At the end of the third year, Eastman had a formula that worked. By 1880, he had invented and patented not only the dry plate, but also a machine for preparing large numbers of plates. He quickly recognized the opportunities with making dry plates for sale to other photographers.

1885    Eastman developed a thin, flexible base film emulsion (Kodak).

1886    Eastman became the first American industrialist to employ a full-time research scientist to aid in the commercialization of his flexible transparent film base. Nicephore Niepce of 1826, the creator of the world's first photograph (Azarmi 1973). The development of the flexible transparent film base solved both Edison's and Eastman's problems. It was the opportunity Edison was waiting for to patent the kinetograph motion picture camera and a separate viewing device called the kinetoscope (Fry and Fourzon 1977). Eastman and Edison collaborated to make motion picture possible. According to Barnouw (1981), the kinetoscope, a product of Thomas Edison and his co-workers, particularly William Kennedy Laurie Dickson, made its debut in 1894—the year before the debut of cinematography. These devices were closely related, and the kinetoscope made "viewing pictures" a reality for peepshow visitors.

1888    George Méliès, a renowned stage magician and director got his start when the Theatre Robert-Houdin was offered for sale, which he purchased with his inheritance. With his established theatre in France, Méliès was now referred to as a theatre manager rather than an artist.

1895    By this time, twenty cinematography machines were developed as a result of various contributions and the combined efforts of the pioneers. These machines were projectors that could also serve as cameras or printing machines.

1895    Méliès later obtained a film stock and a projector from Robert Paul. He used it to start his film career and created over 500 short films in his career.

1897    Méliès accidentally discovered stop-motion. He discovered trick photography when he was filming the Place de L'Opera in Paris. While filming this project, Méliès' camera jammed. It

*The Great Train Robbery*
Directed by Edwin S. Porter

took him a few moments to clear the obstruction and begin filming. "After he had developed the film and was screening it at home, he observed the startling transition that the jammed camera had caused with the scene that he had been filming" (Schechter and Everitt 1980 p. 17). Not long after this incident, Méliès began to experiment with trick photography including fast and slow motion, double exposure, multiple exposures, stop-motion, the dissolve, and the fade. He created several films with the stop-motion technique. In *Cinderella* (1899), Méliès used stop-motion to turn a pumpkin into a coach and grimy rags into a glittering ball gown. Slow motion allowed dancers to hang suspended in mid-air for a longer period of time as they drifted easily towards the earth. Fast and reverse action added touches of slapstick to a still genteel medium. This film saved his theatre from a slow death by boredom and became the sensation of the day and almost single-handedly pulled the business out of a two-year depression. In another film, *A Trip to the Moon* (1902), Méliès used his usual camera tricks, plus close-up, zoom, and the like. In *Great Train Robbery* (1979), American filmmaker and story pioneer Edwin S. Porter illustrated a more practical side to the use of trick effects. In this film, the use of visual effects was extremely subtle and "for the first time in the movies visual effects were used not as a form of spectacle, but as a way of making scenes in a film look natural and lifelike" (Schechter and Everitt 1980 pp. 32-33).

1906    Norman O. Dawn, an American film pioneer, was also a great innovator of camera tricks used to fake reality. His love for visual effects and film began in 1906, when he traveled to Paris where he studied art. Dawn began production on a short film documentary titled *Mission of California* (1907). During the filming of this documentary, Dawn, for the first time in his film career, adapted a still photographic technique known as "glass shot." While filming on location, some of the buildings he was asked to shoot were in poor locations and were surrounded by telephone poles and wires. This problem gave Dawn the opportunity to experiment with glass painting techniques and allowed him to combine his background in painting and photography. He painted trees onto clear glass and used the trees to hide the telephone poles, thus using visual effects techniques as a practical means of improving reality. Dawn was able to use the techniques applied in this assignment to other films to make life look better than it actually was. He is considered a prototype of the modern effects technician, the motion picture craftsman who brings artistry, engineering skill, and boundless ingenuity to the task of performing the impossible.

1911    Norman O. Dawn devised a new and superior way of producing composite images called an "in-the-camera matte shot" and later worked with and developed many other effects techniques, including rear projection (Schechter and Everitt 1980).

### Frame-by-Frame: Development of Stop-motion Animation

Willis O'Brien, who appeared to be comfortable with stop-motion animation, may have gained this confidence through his earlier film production shorts. O'Brien began his animation career at the Edison company and in 1914 created his first stop-motion short called *Dinosaur and The Missing Link*. Ten more shorts followed, each costing $500, and by 1919 *The Ghost of Slumber Mountain* grossed $100,000. After successfully designing the miniature dinosaurs, O'Brien presented it to producer Herbert Dawley, who later patented the design of the dinosaur in 1920. His move to patent the dinosaur structure made it difficult for others who wanted to create dinosaurs.

By the beginning of the 1920s, stop-motion animation was being integrated into film. In 1922, Willis O'Brien created stop-motion animation for a film called "The Lost World," a film based on a novel by Sir Arthur Conan Doyle, the author of the Sherlock Holmes mysteries. Sir Arthur was excited about the 3-D, stop-motion animation that was done by a relatively unknown special effects artist named Willis O'Brien. *The Lost World* showed several dinosaurs fighting in a prehistoric setting. Sir Arthur's showing of the reel caused the news of the film to make the front page of the New York Times. The film made its debut in 1925 and is generally credited as the first full-length film to depend on model animation.

This film was the first of eight film projects that O'Brien would make with model maker Marcel Delgado, a young Mexican sculptor student.

After completing *The Lost World*, O'Brien added to the challenge by creating *King Kong* in 1933. This film used numerous techniques to blend stop-motion animation with live action footage. Two separate Kongs were created; one consisted of a make-up man in a monkey suit running around a scaled-down set, and the second, a full-scale mechanical giant ape. Kong turned out to be a remarkable success for O'Brien, the mechanical effects artist, and others who worked on the project. For O'Brien, in particular, the project marked the end of his second feature film. This film brought him the prestige of being the first animator to integrate such a large mechanical monster successfully into a story that not only focused on the animation, but also on the main actress, Fay Wray.

One audience member who was astounded by the 50-foot mechanical ape was Ray Harryhausen. After viewing the film, the young Harryhausen sought out O'Brien and became his assistant. Harryhausen was only thirteen when he first saw *King Kong,* but this movie changed his life forever. He later made a name for himself through his work as an animator for Willis O'Brien "...on *Mighty Joe Young,* which won O'Brien the Academy Award for special effects in 1949" (Culhane 1981 p. 65). Harryhausen moved up from his apprenticeship position. "The first film on which Harryhausen had control of the special effect was *The Beast from 20,000 Fathoms* (1953), directed by Eugene Lourie from a 'Saturday Evening Post' story by Ray Bradbury" (Culhane 1981 p. 65). Harryhausen had worked on 80% of the animation for O'Brien's *Mighty Joe Young* and felt confident about his work.

Most art historians agree that one of the best mechanical monsters made in the early days of visual effects for the movies was a representation of the dragon "Fafner" built for Fritz Lang's silent classic *Siegfried* (Schechter and Everitt 1980). After witnessing the failure of Douglas Fairbanks' 1924 version of *The Thief of Bagdad*—a film that attempted to use a baby alligator in a dragon disguise for a part in the story that required a mechanical dragon--Lang had designed a 60-foot mechanical reptile. However, Lang's mechanical reptile was just a slightly different operational design from that of Méliès *Frost Giant*. "Four men, standing inside the body of the sixty-foot reptile, operated its neck, head, and tail, while five more, hidden in a trench underneath the dragon's body, moved it along a track built into the fake forest floor" (Schechter and Everitt 1980 p. 153). Lang would have altered the mechanical effects used by Méliès when building his dragon, but future artists were able to improve on what he and Méliès started. In 1933, Willis O'Brien patented his design of a miniature rear-projection system (Hutchison 1987).

Puppet animation as in *King Kong,* created an effects category of its own. Different from that of O'Brien's miniature dinosaurs, puppet animation excludes the use of real-time figures such as hand puppets. Like most techniques in visual effects, its exact point of origin is uncertain, but it began outside the United States. Canley and Korkis write, "Though not common in the United States, puppet animation is recognized and encouraged in Europe and the East. In puppet animation, most puppets have an armature of wood, metal, or wire. This armature is a skeleton that allows the puppet to move slightly at body joints like elbows and knees and maintain that position while it is being photographed. To achieve different expressions, the animators often change the head on the puppets" (p. 101). George Pat was one of the puppet animators who migrated to the United States. He created acclaimed puppet animation in the 1930s and 1940s and later won several Academy Awards in 1943 for "the development of novel methods and techniques" of puppet animation. In later years, he would attract apprentices like Jim Danforth, who was nominated for an Oscar for the visual effects in George Pat's 1964 MGM production of *Seven Faces of Dr. Lao* (Culhane 1981; Cawley and Korkis 1990).

Walt Disney's production of *Snow White and the Seven Dwarfs* (1938) marked the start of a new direction for animation and feature films. Before Disney's production of *Snow White and the Seven Dwarfs*, most major innovations in traditional special effects such as glass shots, matte shots, background painting, mechanical effects, puppets and miniatures, rear-screen and front-screen projection, and optical printer and traveling mattes were explored by various artists on a large scale. A large number of minor visual effects were explored in feature films before Walt Disney's production of *Snow White.* These included effects such as slow motion, time lapse, distortion, the spin, the freeze-frame, reverse movement, and the multiple image effects. Although animation had been explored to a large degree through the stop-motion films of O'Brien, Méliès, and others, these artists explored the techniques of 3-D visual animation effects. Disney was experimenting with the techniques of 2-D visual animation effects, and although there were others experimenting with this technique, it is difficult to know with any degree of certainty who was the first to develop a film using only 2-D animation.

### Early Concepts of Animated Drawings

Before the 1900s, comic strips and cartoons illustrated the concepts of an object and its stages of motion in time. Historians believe this style's origins can be traced back to the cave arts and crafts of various ethnic cultures; such illustrations can be found in an Egyptian wall decoration circa 2000 B.C. In successive panels, the wall decorations depict two Egyptian wrestlers struggling in a variety of holds. Other developments like the lantern shows and shadow plays were presented in a similar form in the late 1830s. For home entertainment, children created these plays through the use of sheets, with human and animal silhouettes, which they pasted onto cardboard and cut out. Shadow plays were only the beginning of animation toys and developed to a level in which they incorporated basic visual effects such as moving clouds, water, and atmospheric effects in the backgrounds of the silhou-

Egyptian wall decoration—shown in the tomb of Prince Bakht. Middle Kingdom, 11th Dynasty 2133-1992 BC.

ettes (Solomon 1989).

In 1826, Peter Mark Roget, the author of *Persistence of Vision with Regard to Moving Objects* began to investigate the "wheel phenomenon." Roget inquired as to "why the spokes of a rapidly spinning wheel seem to turn backward or forward or seem to stand still at different times" (Solomon, 1989, p. 7). In his conclusion, Roget reportedly "...described the important fact that the human eye will blend a series of sequential images into a single motion if the images are presented rapidly, with sufficient illumination, and interrupted regularly" (Solomon, 1989, p. 7). Roget's research into the question of the wheel led to the invention of the phenakistoscope ("an optical deceiver" in Greek) or fantoscope by scientist Joseph Plateau in 1826 or 1828. A more complex device than the thaumatrope, the phenakistoscope was made up of two discs.

Another animated device using similar techniques was the Daedalum or *Wheel of the Devil*, created by William Horner in 1834. In 1860, it was renamed the zoetrope or *Wheel of Life*. The design consisted of a drum that was customized with slits and strips of sequential images placed inside so that when the drum was spun the images seen through the slits appeared to move. The subject matter contained in these short-cycled sequential animation was usually taken from everyday life.

The kineography, invented in 1868, proved to be the least expensive, most durable, and most practical animation toy of its time. The kineography, or flip book as it is called today, consisted of a few dozen drawings or photography of sequential movement bound in order, like the pages of a book. When the book is flipped through rapidly, the images blend and create the illusion of motion. The flipbook was redesigned by Thomas Edison in 1895 and was renamed the mutoscope, a sort of mechanical flipbook. The mutoscope was designed so that the viewer could crank a ring of sequential photographs at greater speeds. Similar inventions followed in 1877 with the advent of the praxinoscope by Emile Reynaud. Reynaud's device was a great improvement to that of his predecessors. He combined his invention with a projector and began drawing animated stories, first on long strips of paper, then on celluloid. This technique of drawing directly onto the film stock was revolutionary and was later repeated in the 1930s by animators such as Len Lye and Norman McLaren. Although the praxinoscope used similar principles of the kineograph, there was one distinct difference between them: "...the praxinoscope was not an animated toy but film" (Solomon 1989).

Various experiments of visual perception were conducted long before the 1900s, but true animation could not be achieved until people understood a fundamental principle of the human eye: the persistence of vision.

1899    Eadweard Muybridge's efforts later culminated in the two volumes *Animation in Motion* (1899) and *The Human Figure in Motion* (1901).

1905    Emile Cohl pioneered the art of 2-D animation on film. In 1905, he experimented with single-frame exposures of cartoons, and later he set out to make a film in which each frame was a

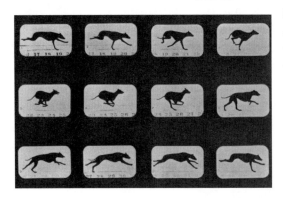

separate photograph of individual drawings. He altered the drawing slightly from one frame to the other to imitate live-action film. His first cartoon animation, titled *Mr. Stop*, was the first known to use the technique of frame-to-frame drawings.

1906    James Stuart Blackton was an early animation pioneer whose first project was completed in 1906. Blackton was born in England and immigrated to the United States as an infant.

Eadweard Muybridge, Greyhound Running, 1879

Blackton became interested in the possibilities of frame-by-frame film making. He filmed an amusing project called *Humorous Phase of Funny Faces*. Often viewed as America's first animator, he continued to experiment with the medium of film, but his next film *The Haunted Hotel* (1907) contained only 3-D stop-motion techniques and was viewed as a success in America and Europe. Blackton was a known inventor and innovator but lost interest in animation by the year 1910. He may have become busy with his job as supervisor of all the company production at Vitagraph or may have tired of the medium itself.

1926    Blackton sold the company, Vitagraph to Warner Brothers.

## Winsor McCay: A Unique Style of Movement

New York became the melting pot for poor European immigrants between 1900 and 1910. George McManus was one of these immigrants. A cartoonist famous for the Maggie and Jiggs comic strip, he developed a short cartoon using his characters. He showed his film at the New York Herald after working hours. The movements of the characters impressed all the workers, with the exception of his lifelong friend and cartoonist Winsor McCay. McCay believed that he could draw the frames faster and better than his friend George. The men agreed to a bet on the spot. After the bet was made by George, who challenged McCay to do twice the amount of work in the same amount of time, McCay increased the challenge by agreeing to draw in a background as well. Later, McCay developed his first animation Little Nemo based on his famous newspaper comic. He drew close to 4,000 separate drawings for a film that lasted about three minutes and was considered the longest animation to date. As promised, McCay even included background, which he reused from one drawing to the other. He won the bet and collected on it that evening.

    McCay was interested in film animation even before

Frames from *Le Retapeur de cervelles* (Brains Repaired, 1911), by French animator Emile Cohl

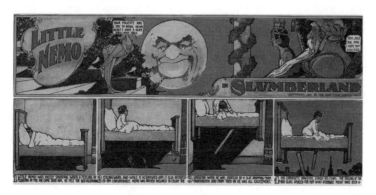

Winsor McCay 1905, *Little Nemo*

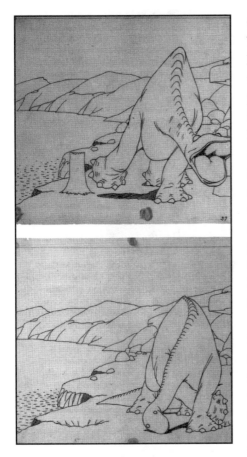

Gertie the Dinosaur, created by McCay.

George McManus showed his animation at the New York Herald. In fact, his son Winsor McCay Jr. first led him in that direction. While he and his father waited to cross a busy street in New York City, McCay Jr. picked up a flipbook on the street and excitedly showed it to his father. But instead of giving the toy to his son, McCay pocketed it for himself. He later studied the sequences photographed in the flip book. He used Indian ink on translucent rice paper and timed movement to a split second with a stopwatch. He not only refined the movements but also hand tinted each frame to match the colors of the comic strip. His first film premiered in April 1911. His second film was more technical and was entitled *How a Mosquito Operates*, but this film was not an improvement on his first attempt.

His third film, *Gertie the Dinosaur*, was his most famous animation. Gertie was done with excellent draftsmanship, which caused most to believe that he might have traced it from a photograph. This animation formed the foundation of character animation, the art of delineating a character's personality through a unique style of movement. McCay communicated Gertie's endearing and somewhat childish personality by paying close attention, for example, to the angles at which she tilted her head to listen to other characters or flicked her tail to disobey. By this time, audiences were beginning to realize that they were seeing a new art form develop—one that used drawings to communicate a story on film. Among McCay's audiences were a number of young men who were so impressed by what they saw that they decided to become animators, including Walter Lantz, Dave Fleischer, and Dick Huemer.

1913    The first studio, the Raoul Barre Studio, opened in New York. Like most other animators, Raoul Barre began by drawing comics. Other studios were also established by independent animators. But it was John Randolph, a Michigan-born artist and businessman, who truly industrialized the medium to that of an assembly-line production. Randolph employed six animators to work out of his New York apartment.

1914    Earl Hurd patents the celluloid which becomes one of the most important inventions in early animation history.

1919    Eighteen-year-olds Walt Disney and Ub Iwerk began their first business venture which ended months later.

1921    Hurd pioneered a combination of live action with animation. This method was not new to the screen, but Hurd was able to innovate its use in a unique method used in his film, *Johnnie Out of the Inkwell* in 1921.

1922    Ub Iwerk and Walt Disney made a second attempt at starting an independent studio in Kansas City called Laugh-o-grams. The studio went bankrupt two years later. The films were successful, but the company's finances were shaky. Animated cartoons, however simple, were costly to make. They cost between $1,000 and $2,000 for a seven-minute short. Disney insisted on giving the customer the best product possible and began cutting back the slender profits in order to perfect the product. Depressed by his second bankrupt company and disenchanted with Kansas City as a place for business fulfillment, Walt Disney caught a train to California's Orange Grove and the hills of Hollywood in 1923. With his brother Roy Disney as his new partner, Walt later encouraged Ub to work at the studio and promised to pay him $160.00 per month. Iwerks took the offer to come to Hollywood to assist on the *Alice* series (a series of films that integrated live action with cel animation to tell the stories of live actress *Alice* in a cartoon wonderland). At this time, still considered a beginner in the field of animation, Walt Disney produced work that was comparable with the New York animation studios. Others began to follow his style of character design, and by the 1930s Warner Brothers and MGM were unable to rival Disney.

Character developers created animation principles that

were used to train student animators in the art of motion. Today, Disney's principles of animation are well-established and practiced by many animators in the industry. But the contributions of Ub Iwerks were crucial to the development and establishment of these principles. Undoubtedly one of Disney's most creative and valuable animators, Ub Iwerk designed the physical characteristics of Mickey Mouse. He later redesigned the mouse to ease animating. It had been discovered that circular forms were simpler to animate effectively; therefore, Ub's original set of mouse designs took advantage of circles—two large circles represented the trunk and the head. Other smaller circles were added to represent ears, rubber-hose arms, and large circular feet. The gift of personality was probably Disney's own contribution to Mickey. Walt controlled the situations in which the mouse found himself, while allowing the animators freedom to develop and collaborate on how to create its personality.

1928    After the creation of Mickey Mouse and such shorts as *Steamboat Willie* (1928) and the fifty-seven *Alice* comedies (1923 -1927) Disney gained the confidence and capital to produce a full-length feature animation film.

1929    As a result of the rapid developments in the field, Earl Hurd went out of business and found employment at Disney in the early 1930s as a story editor and worked on the production of *Snow White and the Seven Dwarfs*.

The studios were beginning to develop their own characters, which were in most ways improvements on the comic strip characters of the newspapers. The most famous—indeed, internationally famous—character of the 1920s was Felix the Cat. This character was created by Otto Messmer, who discovered the idea for the character after his wife brought a stray alley cat home on a rainy night. After studying the motions and attitudes of the cat, Messmer replicated it and added a human quality to the character. Both Otto Messmer and Pat Sullivan are credited with the development of the cat caricature. Felix followed the successful strip cartoon Krazy

Kat and Ignatz Mouse, a fantasy cartoon, created by George Herriman. Krazy Kat and Felix set the trend for an anthropomorphism in cartoons that reached its peak with Mickey Mouse in the 1930s. His influence on Disney's earlier cartoons is seen in Julius the Cat in the *Alice* series.

1930s   Most corporations such as Warner Brothers, Fox, and RCA made contributions in the area of sound. Most animators were experimenting with sound and color in their animation during the late 1920s. As a result of these developments, live-action pictures developed into small stories, and so did the animated shorts. But these developments also symbolized the growth of what was once a hobby, into an industry. Independent animators now needed to have new, highly complex machinery to compete with the new companies. Although many before had tried, the one company best known for industrializing the art of animation is Walt Disney. Disney is credited with introducing the concept of the storyboard, which allowed for more attention to story structure.

1937    Disney had acquired the confidence and capital required to produce a full-length feature animation film. The result was the color feature *Snow White and the Seven Dwarfs*. The most honored animated film of its time, *Snow White and the Seven Dwarfs* was released to the Christmas time trade in 1937. *Snow White* brought a full feature animation to the movies and combined a great number of techniques that had been used in special effects.

Conclusion
Beyond the traditional effects of the early to mid-1900s, artists and scientists began to work on different techniques for visual effects that incorporated the use of computer technology. Computers had been used in the production of traditional effects before this time. The programmed mechanical arm used to gain precise camera moves is evidence of the integration of computer technology in the field of traditional special effects before the mid-1900s. Beyond its use in traditional special effects, the computer was being developed by computer scientists who were determined

to show other uses for it. Later, these scientists were joined by artists who were determined to create art out of the computer's graphics applications. These artists, interested in computer technology, came from three primary traditional arts backgrounds—traditional fine arts, film, and video. Due to the complexity of this emerging technology, the artists often collaborated with computer scientists to learn about the technology that enabled them to create their art. In chapter three, I will focus on three pioneers, one from each of the disciplines.

# Chapter 4
# Early Influences

**Development of Computer Graphics**

Most of the early computer graphics tools were developed at educational institutions (such as Massachusetts Institute of Technology, Ohio State University, New York Institute of Technology, Cornell, University of Utah, and the University of North Carolina-Chapel Hill) and professional research centers (such as Bell Labs, Boeing, and Xerox). This development lead to the tools that were later used by studios to create computer-generated imagery for movies and television in the 1970s to the present day.

Building on digital technology from the Massachusetts Institute of Technology Whirlwind computer of the late 1940s, early research at Lincoln Laboratory, established in 1951, was focused on the design and prototype development of a network of ground-based radars and aircraft control centers for continental air defense. Significant technical advances supporting this work resulted in the first real-time computer processing of radar data and the development of magnetic-core data storage to greatly increase system reliability and computer memory. Terms such as bit were created by J.W. Tukey, a researcher at AT&T Bell Laboratories during the late 1940s. It was a shorthand way of saying binary digit. A binary is a unit of storage that represents only one of two values, on or off—0 and 1. 1951 also marked the start of the vectorscope graphics display on MIT's Whirlwind computer. It was also in this year that General Motors Research Laboratory began researching the role of computer aided design.

The computer was merely a device used by scientists as a pragmatic solution to an otherwise difficult problem. The difficulty of working with this early device discouraged even the scientists, mathematicians, and engineers who used it. However in 1950, the development of pioneering "oscillons" or "electronic abstractions" sparked the birth of electronic images. Ben F. Laposky, a mathematician and artist from Cherokee, Iowa, created the first graphic image to be generated by an electronic machine. The image was created by manipulating electronic beams across the fluorescent face of an oscilloscope's cathode-ray tube and then recording the abstract patterns using high-speed film, color filters, and special camera lenses. Laposky used an analog device, that naturally creates various patterns. The basic electric wave form is modified in these compositions with different electronic input (Goodman 1987). Analog devices were difficult to program and impossible to control, like a tree grown naturally, it was impossible to predict the growth pattern of its branches.

Digital systems offered more control and wider visual possibilities. The Whirlwind was one of the first computers to use a display screen like a television monitor. The magic of this computer was demonstrated in 1951 on the television show *See It Now*. This demonstration showed a bouncing ball that was created through programmed animation to lose height with every bounce.

The mid-1950s was marked by a flood of small rectangular cards, punched full of holes and imprinted with the warning: "Do not fold, spindle, or mutilate." These IBM cards introduced the average person to the computer and data processing. At this time, a computer hardware that filled a good-size room, and contained tens of thousands of electron tubes requiring enough electricity to power a high-rise office building was the prized possession of government and research organizations (Hutchison 1987 p. 78).

In the mid-to-late 1950s, the SAGE Air Defense System of the United States Air Force was introduced at MIT. Introduced by Ivan Sutherland, this system used command and control cathode ray tube (CRT) displays (Created in 1956 by Bertram Herrzog of the University of Michigan computing center in a study of military vehicle behavior.) with which operators could detect aircraft flying over the continental U.S. It allowed them to obtain information about the aircraft by pointing at their icon on the CRT screen with light pens. During these early stages of the computer's development as an visual medium, its graphics and programming were primarily done by computer scientists. Such early attempts had little impact beyond scientific and technical interest, and were confined to universities. Most of the technological developments came out of government- and academic-research laboratories such as MIT's Lincoln Labs.

In 1956, Lawrence Livermore National Labs connected a graphics display to an IBM 704 mainframe computer. In 1957, IBM created 740-780 computer models. The Defense Department's Advanced Research Project Agency was also founded in this year. In 1957, Russell Kirsch produced the first image-processed picture. This technique was made possible shortly after the debut of the system. A device was created to allow for a method of feeding pictures into a computer by scanning them on a rotating drum with a photoelectric cell and then processing the data in various ways. This device was created by the U.S. National Bureau of Standards on the Standard Eastern Automation Computer system.

By 1958, a filmmaker named John Whitney, Sr. became interested in combining music and graphics. He devised his own computer-assisted mechanism and integrated this with others such as an M-5 anti-aircraft gunfight computer; with this equipment Whitney created visual animation. The animation used an analog computer to control the movement of the artwork and camera.

In 1961 Whitney used this system to create the title sequence for Alfred Hitchcock's film *Vertigo*. He later went on to produce *Catalog*, which led to other feature film projects that allowed him to showcase the various animation effects that were possible using his technique. In 1963-66 he produced *Lapis* with his brother James (Morrison 1994).

At MIT's Lincoln Labs, 1958 saw new researchers, such as Steven Coons, Ivan E. Sutherland, and Timothy Johnson. They began to use the computer system to manipulate drawn pictures.

In 1959, the major output devices were created. The first commercial film recorder was developed in San Diego, California by a company called General Dynamics. CalComp introduced the world's first drum plotter (Model 565). Commercially available, this plotter created a way for artist and designers to print their computer-based drawings. The plotter is a computer-driven mechanical drawing machine capable of delineating linear configurations. The model 565 was capable of printing 12 inches by 1440 inches. The data that the plotter follows are stored in the computer in the form of mathematical coordinates. Also in 1959, DAC-1 (Design Augmented by Computers) became the first computer-aided drawing system, created by Don Hart and Ed Jacks. The drawings were the result of ongoing research at the General Motors Research Lab since it was founded in 1951. The lab used the IBM 7090 and the results could be outputted to 35-mm film or used to control the movement of computer-controlled devices.

William Fetter coined the term "computer graphics" in 1960. A researcher at Boeing Company, the term was first used to describe his computer-generated plotter drawings of an airplane cockpit. In the early 1960s, Fetter collaborated with Walter Bernhart to produce animation of an aircraft carrier landing. Using the plotter, 3-D drawings were plotted on paper and filmed in sequence one at a time like the making of a traditional animation film. Fetter did various animation that included models of humans illustrating his ergonomic design of cockpits.

During this time period when computer graphics were being pioneered, little emphasis was focused on the resulting art. It was more about process, or the means to do it, though "it" was not defined. The field was bombarded with scientists, mathematicians, and technicians who created art as a means of showing off the results of their technological pioneering efforts. The early computer had limited capabilities. Though it excelled in number crunching, the early systems were slow, non-interactive, difficult to program, and even the largest system's memory was limited. Even the scientists (with sometimes huge artistic aspirations) were limited to linear mathematical functions that preformed such tasks as rotate, transform, interpolate, and produce random variations. These early functions were also used on systems such as the flight simulator, CADAM (Computer Aided Design and Manufacturing) systems, the CAT scanners and other systems that were developed to visualize objects and situations that were too costly or impossible to represent through other means.

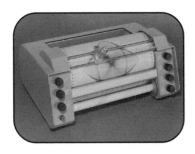

CalComp early plotter courtesy CalComp.

Once the development of computers with the capabilities

to produce graphics was well on the way, the goal then shifted to size and economics. Wesley Clark, principal architect of the TX-0 and TX-2, began pioneering efforts to this end. A proponent of the idea that computers are tools and that convenience of use is the most important single design factor, he began working toward a more affordable and compact system. He later developed two computers, the Average Response Computer (ARC) of 1958 and the Laboratory Instrument Computer (LINC) of the early 1960s. The LINC cost $32,000; at the time, a small price to pay for a system with a 12-bit parallel machine with a 1 kilobit-word memory, an analog to digital converter, a small CRT display made from a modified oscilloscope, and two block addressable drives. Although neither of these systems were designed with the artist in mind, nor used to create art, Clark's theories prefigured the workstation computer revolution of the 1980s, which ultimately benefitted all, including the artists.

A spin-off company of the MIT Lincoln Laboratory, Digital Equipment Design Corp. (DEC) opened in 1957. This company was also interested in compact systems and in 1960 introduced the Programmed Data Processor-1 (PDP); arguably the world's most compact system. DEC was also involved in the development of the LINC. Twenty LINCs were built for biomedical use. By 1963, over 1200 LINC had been manufactured commercially. DEC sold about 150 copies of the LINC-8, a combination of the LINC and the PDP-8, and about 1000 PDP-12s, which incorporated a modified LINC design. John Whitney Sr. founded Motion Graphic, Inc. of Los Angeles in 1960. Whitney was one of a few individuals that became increasingly interested in the computer and its ability to create motion and graphics during the 1960s. Others included Charles Csuri of Ohio State University, Ken Knowlton, A. Michael Noll, Lillian Schwartz, E. E. Zajac, M. Schroeder, and Stan Vanderbeek.

In 1961, the first video game *Spacewar* was developed by MIT student Steve Russell. Written for the DEC PDP-1, this game was an instant success, and copies started flowing to other PDP-1 owners. It was later used by DEC as a diagnostic program for new PDP-1 machines (Morrison 1994). In 1962, Alan Kotok and Bob

Ivan Sutherland working on Sketchpad

Sanders constructed a joystick that was used with the PDP-1 to control the spaceships in *Spacewar*.

In 1962, Ivan Sutherland of MIT Lincoln Laboratory developed the first interactive graphics program called the *Sketchpad*. A graduate student, Sutherland developed the program as part of his thesis published in 1963 entitled *Sketchpad: A Man-Machine Graphical Communications System*. This was originally designed to assist mechanical and electrical designers who needed a tool to speed up the traditional process of hand-drawn designs. The Sketchpad system was designed on the TX-2 computer, a large-scale, transistorized digital computer designed to input and output experiments such as the Sketchpad. This system, created in the late 1950s, was the advancement of the TX-0. The Sketchpad allowed the user to draw directly onto the CRT screen with an input device known as the light pen. The user utilized a system of push buttons and switches to give the computer such direct commands as delete a line, move a point, and scale or rotate a line. With a zoom factor of 2000 to 1 and a maximum page size of quarter of a mile, the user could detail the various parts of the drawing with great precision. Later, other input devices such as the tablet were added to the TX-2.

### Charles Csuri: An Approach to Early Computer Art

Born on July 4, 1922, in the small coal-mining community of Grant Town, West Virginia, Csuri went to high school in Cleveland. His family moved there after his father, a West Virginia coal miner, was injured in the mines. The idea of an artistic career never entered Csuri's mind during his high school days. He was planning to become an industrial engineer and majored in mechanical drawing and machine shop work with this end in view (Jacobs and Roberts March 1947). But young Csuri enjoyed drawing and took drawing lessons at the Cleveland Art Museum.

Arriving at The Ohio State University in 1940, his original plans for industrial engineering were soon pushed into the background. One day, he idly made a sketch of a friend and was gratified to find the likeness very good. Following up this new-found talent, he enrolled in a drawing course, during which he received so much encouragement he soon decided to change his major (Jacobs and Roberts, March 1947). The artist, who in his earlier days copied Rembrandt as a form of practice, now found himself digging deeper and becoming aware of different methods.

After earning a master's degree in fine arts, Csuri, who had taught sculpture as a graduate student, joined The Ohio State University faculty and settled into teaching, drawing, and painting. For about ten years, he worked in various modes—some expressionistic, others surrealistic, still others conceptual—and in different media, even combining painting and sculpture (Hall April 1990). His work with palette and brush was readily accepted; he held one-man shows in New York City, yet in 1964, Csuri decided to turn the computer into an artist's tool (Trachtman February 1995). He became increasingly fascinated by the applications of the computer to art. Studying computer programming in his spare time, he began using mathematical concepts in his art. The computer he was using at the time was a huge mainframe that required data entry on punched cards. Csuri had to become a programmer in order to communicate with the computer and so he enrolled in a computer-programming course (Trachtman February 1995).

As a professor in the School of Arts, Csuri pondered the results of a visual form of mathematical systems that were used to examine the various aspects of his sketches. He teamed up with James Shaffer, an engineer and programmer at the University's Computer Center, to find the answer that lay in the heart of the giant computers. Both men were interested in a mathematical approach to art—especially those mathematical variations that resulted in forms impossible to visualize ahead of time. The computer enabled them to exploit unique capabilities to process the visual data and to approach problems of artistic content in a new way. Csuri admits that many of the drawings that the computer produced in the early days were not difficult to copy, but it was the concept more than the draw-

*Sine Curve Man* created by Csuri and Shaffer, 1966

Hummingbird created by Charles Csuri, 1967. In 1963 he became the first artist to use the computer as a means of reproducing his pencil-drawn sketches. Csuri input is drawings into the computer and assigned coordinates to the outlines. The coordinates were then transformed to create variations of the original hand-drawn art and were output through a plotter.

ings that were important. For example, Csuri made a simple drawing of a man's face. A grid of X and Y lines is then set over the face, and the points of each line are numbered. Those numbers then go onto computer cards.

Csuri's willingness to embrace this new and uncertain art form angered members of his traditional Fine arts Department. Csuri was in discord with the department and the university moved him from the Department of Fine arts to the more tolerant Department of Art Education, with a joint appointment as professor of computer science.

Csuri and Shaffer worked on the process for about nine months and had created more than 300 drawings ("Artists" April 1967). In 1967, the arts and programming efforts resulted in the Sine Curve Man, a face drawn in line art and distorted with a mathematical sine curve equation. In another piece, Csuri produced distortions of faces, bodies, and limbs, all capitalizing on the computer's knack for varying themes more rapidly and precisely than an artist. In another Csuri drawing, Hummingbird, the computer generated 14,000 variations of one form. The animated film picks apart the drawn bird, scatters it around the screen, and then puts it back together. The Museum of Modern Art in New York City bought the film in 1968 for its permanent collection ("Chuck" n.d.). In that same year, Csuri changed his focus as a faculty member at the university. After seeing what the computer could do and the great deal of potential it had in the area of visual arts, Csuri focused more on the area of computer graphics and animation.

The National Science Foundation sponsored his work in the field for 25 years. During this span of time, Csuri obtained $7 million in federal research grants to the research group, and occasional small projects were sponsored by private industry. With project assignments sponsored by the U.S. Naval Equipment Training Center, Csuri's research group (Computer Graphics Research Group CGRG) developed realistic looking buildings and trees on the computer. The detailed scenes were used in flight simulators to help train pilots. The relatively simple graphics provided pilots with more visual cues than were available to them before.

As the computer graphics industry developed, Csuri altered his approach. He always viewed the computer as the latest in a long series of technical breakthroughs and admitted that he exploited this new medium for its expressive potential. In the computer's 3-D environment, he used this tool to mimic painting—the look of heavy thick paint or impasto, in which the brush marks trail off. Csuri's traditional art education allowed him to emphasize the dichotomy between two and three dimensions in his work. His background as both a painter and sculptor gave him the practical knowledge of visualizing 2-D images in the round (Hall April 1990). But his experimental side is dominant and his style constantly evolves. Throughout his development, computers have enabled Csuri to sculpt images in three dimensions, view them from any angle, set them in motion, and alter them in ways that often blur the distinctions between special effects and art.

The Computer Graphics Research Group brought together graduate students with interests in programming, filmmaking, and visual arts. The programmers and artists of the research group developed proprietary software and worked with systems such as the Anima II. This computer system was designed to produce 3-D, real-time, realistic key-frame animation. The group used this program for various projects ranging from helping deaf children understand language arts to showing college students the effects of a near collision of galaxies in space. CGRG also developed the computer program that was later used in the climax to the Star Wars movie—the trench scene on the Death Star. In July 1986, Csuri established the Advanced Computing Center for the Arts and Design (ACCAD) at The Ohio State University (OSU), an expansion of the earlier research group. Built on OSU's history of collaboration between artist and scientist, ACCAD is a nucleus for students with backgrounds in the arts, mathematics, computer information science, and industrial design.

In 1982, Csuri helped found Cranston-Csuri Productions, a private computer graphics and animation company that

3D computer image courtesy Charles Csuri. Hand painted textures are mapped onto 3D computer geometry

specialized in the field of visual effects for television commercials. His company produced animation for ABC and CBS, NBC Sports, CBS Superbowl XVIIII, and commercials for TRW, Sony, and General Electric. Csuri also had a keen interest, very early, in the development of computer imagery that could be used for scientific visualization.

Scientists at Bell Telephone Laboratories in New Jersey made the first major step towards wider usage of computers in the early-1960s. Ken Knowlton, a Ph.D. graduate of the Electronic Engineering Department of MIT joined the research team at Bell Labs in 1962. "At Bell Labs we had a microfilm printer that exposed a reel of film by the reader typing characters or drawing lines so that suggested to several of us that we could make movies," Knowlton describes. The equipment was not designed as a movie-making device and the absence of pin registration resulted in unusable movie quality. Knowlton describes the graphics environment at the Labs: "Some other guys were doing more specific projects, wondering how a satellite tumbles in space and educational films, Newton's law of gravity. I was more into the more general question of devising a language for creating animated movies." The programming language BEFLIX, the first animation program of 1963 was the result of Knowlton's scientific experiments. Later, other facilities developed their own languages for creating programmed animation. The advent of input devices such as the mouse, created by Doug Englebart, and the digitizing tablet introduced by Colin Hilton created the possibilities for the computer user to draw. Several experimental artists and animators were also becoming interested in the use of these early computer graphics. Their primary goal was to develop the aesthetic and perceptual dimensions of their work. These artists applied their prior art knowledge to the evolution of the new technology; therefore, the artists who worked with technology during this early stage did not abandon their traditional art skills; instead, they viewed computers as tools that allowed them to extend the bounds of their creativity.

Bell Labs was a free environment that allowed researchers to focus on various areas of technological development. In 1962, while summer interning at this facility with the "very best technology of the day," A. Michael Noll became interested in the uses of the computer in generating art. "I still can remember the day when a fellow summer intern, Elwyn Berlekamp, came down the hallway with a computer generated plot of data that had gone astray because of some program error," Noll said. Noll, a scientist who always had a deep interest in art and stereoscopy immediately began thinking of the possibilities of generating abstract computer art. "The lines went every which way all over his plots" he said. "It then occurred to me to use this computer, an IBM 7090, and the Stromberg Carlson plotter to create computer art deliberately." He created several works using this technique, but credits *Gaussian-Quadratic* as his first computer generated art image. He later underwent a successful struggle with the Copyright Office at the Library of Congress to copyright the image as what is perhaps the first registered piece of art produced with a digital computer.

1963 had its share of introductions, such as the first sponsored computer art competition organized by the Computers and Automation Magazine. John Lansdown pioneered the use of computers as an aid to architectural planning with the introduction of his own computer aided design program. With his program, he was able to visualize buildings, elevators, and plot sunlight cast on buildings. Working at the Computer Institute of The Stuttgart, polytechnic Frieder Nake produced four-color drawings through the use of a plotter drawing machine, called the Graphomat Z use Z64. Developments were made in the area of computer graphics mapping systems.

In 1964, Noll was officially transferred into the research department at Bell Labs. In 1965, scientist George Nees of Bell Labs arranged for the first show of computer images at the Technishe Hocschule in Stuttgrat, West Germany. That same year, the first exhibition of computer images was held at the Howard

A. Michael Noll, 1965 *Computer Composition with Lines*

A. Michael Noll, 1965 *Guassian Quadratic*, 11 x 8.5"

Wise Gallery in New York City. Here, the scientists displayed works drawn by a microfilm plotter, conceived by Noll and Bela Julesz at Bell Labs. As expected, the show was not well-received by the art critics. Stuart Perston, an art critic from the *New York Times* wrote "The wave of the future crashes significantly at the Howard

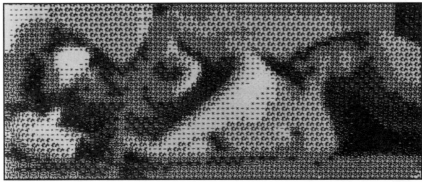

Wise Gallery. The show merely provided proof of the potential for computer-generated art, as the scientists were more interested in what a computer can be programmed to do rather than the art.

*Nude* (Study in Perception) 1966, created by Kenneth Knowlton and Leon Harmon. Original 30 x 144"

1965 also saw the invention of *video art*, a term that was created by Korean artist Nam June Paik.

By the mid-1960s, Leon Harmon and Kenneth Knowlton, researchers at Bell Labs, created *Study in Perception, Nude*. The piece was created as a means of answering several question posed by Knowlton: "How visible must it be? Why do we see something from far away? With most things, the closer you get, the better you can see it and here is something you can see as an overall image from far away but yet still it doesn't really consist of much. How minimal can it be? What is the maximum surprise you can get by making an image out of a small number of things?" The technique used a program to convert the shades of a black and white images to symbols. First, a slide of the original image is scanned into the computer and the whites, blacks, and grays are translated into various symbols of appropriate densities. The two worked on a series of images entitled *Studies in Perception*. Using this technique of density, their chief goal was to investigate the amount of information needed to convey an image.

Knowlton collaborated with various artists at Bell Labs, including Stan VanDerBeek between 1964 and 1970. "Stan VanDerBeek and I got to working together through a mutual friend,

Peter Neumann," Knowlton said. Admittedly, his relationship with the artist was often technically exhausting. "I was the programmer and they did the artistic parts of coloring, cutting, snipping and adding sound and we had lots of suggestions back and forth. With VanDerBeek and in most cases, it was difficult," Knowlton explains. "VanDerBeek was just full of ideas. He would come for half the day every week and I would be exhausted by the end of that day." But Knowlton had a limited set of tools and methods, and efforts to program VanDerBeek's changing visions were difficult.

Later, in 1968, he worked with artist Lillian Schwartz who went on to create a number of images, some of which were influenced by this concept. Schwartz, who was already working with various technologies became intrigued by the *Study in Peception, Nude* that was exhibited along side her work, *Proxima Centauri*, in the 1968 Museum of Modern Art Show. "At the show I met Leon," Schwartz recalls, "and Leon invited me to the lab. I was there for many months before I met Ken." Schwartz worked initially with John Vollaro, at the time Harmon's assistant. "John was very instrumental in me learning the computer punch tape and making symbols," Schwartz said. Schwartz eventually met Knowlton who showed her what was possible with the BEFLIX move system through a screening of his animated films. After viewing the films, Schwartz remarked to Knowlton, "They are very limiting," Schwartz said "and I gave all negative comments." The result of this conversation and interaction led to *Explore*, a new program created by Knowlton.

Knowlton later created several other mosaic type works, with different mediums including shells, found objects and words that were used to answer similar questions to that of *Studies in Perception*

In 1966, *Odyssey*, the first home video game was created at Sanders Associates by a supervising engineer called Ralph Baer. 1966 was also the year that Ivan Sutherland, a former MIT Student, now associate professor at Harvard and students created the first head-mount display called *The Sword of Damocles*, the device displayed a set of wire-frame images for each eye. Mean-

"If art bothers you then it is really good."

—Manfred Mohr

while in Canada, the International Conference on Design and Planning, Computers in Design and Communication, was founded and held its first conference, which was organized by professors Constant and Krampen, at the University of Waterloo in Canada.

E.A.T. Experiments in Art and Technology

In 1966, Billy Klüver, an engineer at Bell Labs who by then had already collaborated with such artists as Jean Tinguely, Robert Rauschenburg, Jasper Johns, and Andy Warhol, had successfully organized 10 artists and 40 engineers for an event called 9 Evenings: Theatre and Engineering. Held at the 69th Regiment Armory in New York City, the performances drew an audience of over 10,000. "Bell Labs was a unique place," Klüver recalls, "I had to ask my boss to come and see what I was doing and you could work on your own and that's why they allowed me to do what I was doing to work with the artist." The resulting show proved his belief in the collaboration of art and science. "Robert Rauschenburg and I decided that something must be done," Klüver recalls "because the artist was cut off from technology; they did not have access to it." It is with that problem in mind that Billy Klüver and fellow Bell Labs engineer Fred Waldhauer, and artists Robert Rauschenburg and Robert Whitman founded the Experiments in Art and Technology (E.A.T.) in New York City in 1967. The opening meeting was held at Rauschenburg's studio, and was well attended. Rauschenburg an artist, and Klüver a engineer at Bell Labs were interested in uniting artists and engineers for the purpose of creating art. "We had a system for matching artists with engineers. We recruited engineers who wanted to work with artists," Klüver said. "We thought that the best way for the artist to be introduced to the technology was through an engineer, not to begin from fear and try to build up some knowledge, but to work with an engineer, to collaborate."

One example of a successful relationship between artist and scientist was VanDerBeek and Knowlton. "Klüver and E.A.T.

used VanDerBeek and I as an example for what they were trying to do," Knowlton explained. By the time E.A.T. was established, the two men were already lecturing about their collaborations at various university venues. At E.A.T., members soon
realized that art and science were not mutually exclusive areas
of specialization. "Conflict inevitably arose between the artists
and the scientists, and just as some of the scientists declared
that they were artists, some of the artists claimed substantial
scientific knowledge" (Schwartz 1992). Throughout the conflicts, the artists and scientists had the opportunity to present
research on their areas of specialization in the form of group
lectures. By the 1970s, the organization had over six thousand
members, but began to wane as the medium became more popular.

Perhaps the mood of E.A.T. is best described by Knowlton
in a lecture given at E.A.T. in 1968 where he expressed his
concerns and interest. He felt that people should be obliged to
try to use at least a part of the new machinery deliberately to
make the environment more beautiful and inspiring through
new forms of computer design. He credits the computer for its
role in blending the details, symmetries, regularities, random-
ness, textures, and richness that were otherwise impossible to
achieve. "The computer," he explained, "helps us to appreciate,
understand, and enhance our humanity." He believes that our
success in this arena will be aided psychologically by our ability to perceive the computer as a friend and as an instrument
not necessarily of regimentation but one which can help us
significantly to experience and assert our humanity" (Russett
and Starr 1988 p.193).

E.A.T. influenced others to work toward its philosophy
of collaboration among the arts and sciences. At MIT, the Center for Advanced Visual Studies was founded by Gyorgy Kepes
in 1967. Influenced by E.A.T.'s mission, the Center provided a
collaborative environment for the artists and scientists to assist
each other. In England, Aland Sutliffe founded the Computer
Arts Society with a similar mission. The organization published
a newsletter called Page to share writings and events that were

of interest to the arts community. In 1969, a branch of the society was founded in America by Kurt Lauckner.

Events of the late 1960s confirmed the establishment of computers in the arts. With growing public interest in technological art, exhibitions were curated to show, not only the art, but also how the technology worked. In 1967, an English artist, Eduardo Paolozzi, created a body of work to express his fascination with the technology. The work titled *Universal Electronic Vacuum*, consisted of ten screen prints. "Pontus Hultén's *Machine* exhibition was a broad technological survey designed to signal the end of the machine era and announce the new electronic age" (Goodman 1987). This exhibition called *The Computer and the Arts* was curated by Jasia Reichardt at the London Institute of Contemporary Art in 1968.

Motion capture system is demonstrated at a trade show in 1968. Cover of Audio-Visual Communications. Courtesy Ed Tajchman and Dave Sieg

The show that included all forms of technological art, from poetry and film to robots, and painting, successfully "demonstrated how pervasive the use of advanced technology had become in the creative process" (Goodman 1987). A number of artists' and scientists' works were exhibited in *Cybernetic Serendipity* including Charles Csuri, Lloyd Summers, Robert Mallary, and Duane Palyka. In 1968, Maurice Tuchman, the curator of the Los Angeles County Museum of Art, developed the Art and Technology Program. His plans were to bring together the best technology and match it with great artists. He accepted proposals from the artists. The artists were placed in residence at some of the leading technological corporations in Los Angeles who would sponsor the projects. A combined total of seventy-six artists and corporations participated in the program, so that it became a landmark in the promotion of technology in the arts.

The computer imagery initially referred to as "computer controlled displays" in the 1950s had taken on a new name "information displays," in the early 1960s, along with the establishment of the Society for Information Displays. "The early problem for people who wanted to get involved was that there was no software," says Carl Machover. "They paid a quarter of a million dollars for the display systems and the only display was the power

button which lit up red, so they had to write their own software."
Later, it would be called Computer Graphics and more software
became commercially available that augmented the traditional
hardware driven environment.

John Whitney, Sr.: Early Digital Films

John Whitney is acknowledged as one of the pioneers of independent computer-generated, non-representational films. In
1952, he wrote, produced, and directed engineering films on
guided missile projects for Douglas Aircraft. John Whitney was
best known as an experimenter and technical innovator in the
field of computer-generated films. He photographed the evolution of programmed abstract patterns with the aid of either a
digital or analog computer. He also designed and built his own
specialized equipment that he used to produce his animated
films. Whitney had a keen interest in animating typography
and various forms of abstract designs and invented a mechanical analog computer to aid in this venture. In 1960, Whitney
founded Motion Graphics Inc., a company whose primary goal
was to produce graphics for motion picture and television commercial titles (Russett and Starr 1988). In an interview, Whitney
explained his methodology for advancing from music and film
to the incorporation of computer graphics medium.

Throughout his early years, Whitney studied both music and film informally in the United States and Paris. In fact,
between his experiments with the camera as a child and his
close association with Arnold Schöenberg's apprentice, René
Liebowitz, Whitney gathered a wealth of knowledge on the aspects of these arts.

By the time Whitney had returned to California, he
was excited by the idea of making films that used traditional
art tools such as the airbrush and techniques such as masking
and stenciling for the basis of the film's abstraction. With the
assistance of his brother James, Whitney began the process of
using geometric shapes and meticulous layout designs for creating his art.

Like most artists who are trained to achieve a particular art or master a particular tool—whether it is a traditional tool or contemporary computer software— Whitney took great pride in the process used to achieve the final medium and continue in search of that direct medium. Whitney explains that the art of creating his abstractions comprised ten steps:

> I would fill out the shape. Then there was a possibility of using the negative, so I would put down the negative stencil of that shape and I would blow just a little bit around one corner and then air brush after around, until it completely enveloped that shape. So I had the shape in a positive form and a negative form, and the motion generated by these cards was quite a lively motion with a front edge that would fade out characteristic of airbrush. So, just from that simple technique, I had a whole library of all these different airbrush sequences. They added up to about one hundred fifty to two hundred cards. (p. 181)

Soon, Whitney began building his own equipment for the purpose of creating his films. He was able to expand on the optical printing techniques that were being used by filmmakers for the creation of special-effects films. But throughout his artwork, he paid close attention to details and documentation of the process.

Very early in Whitney's career in the arts, he developed and redesigned the visual effects tools. As Whitney advanced from abstract airbrush film to computer graphics abstract films, he continued to alter his tools.

John Whitney often worked with his brother James. Together, they began working on films. The two also had a keen interest in sound. Funded by a Guggenheim Fellowship over a two-year period, Whitney continued to develop more creative and different ways to create with the new technology. He worked

on a project called The Five Abstraction Film Exercise up until
the late 1940s. During this time,
Whitney became increasingly interested in real-time animation
techniques as opposed to cel animation. He used superimposing
techniques and shot the project on
film. In his paper-cuts, real-time
motion was spontaneous as he
animated them to classic jazz at
the same speed at which they were
replayed to the viewer. Often, he
completed a three-minute film in
an afternoon. He created films such as Dizzy Gillespie Hothouse
through the use of this technique. Confident of his new art
technique, Whitney wrote a proposal to the University of California, Los Angeles, to work with light shows.

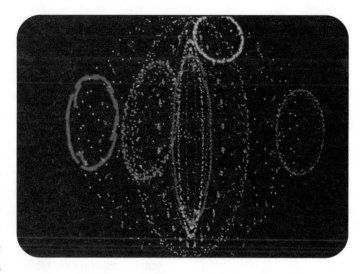

Still frame from *Permutations* (1967) by
John Whitney

Whitney worked on the mechanical-optical machine
between 1958 and 1966. He used the machine to generate funds,
as the machine was in demand. Whitney said, "It became quite
successful. I did a number of commercials and feature film titles
and titles for television shows, using that equipment" (p. 184).
But in addition to being used in various commercial films, a
similar machine was engineered with Whitney's aid, which was
used for his brother's film, Lapis. Whitney explained why this
became James Whitney's final film.

> IBM awarded him a three-year research grant,
> which enabled him to embark on an extensive
> study of motion design using the IBM System
> 3600, a digital computer. The first artistically
> cohesive film that he produced with this sys-
> tem was Permutations, a beautifully composed
> abstract animated work in which he employs
> complicated forms of visual counterpoint. (p.
> 180)

Frame from Lapis 1963-1966
by James Whitney

In the late 1970s, Whitney got access to the computers at Triple I and invited Larry Cuba to work with him as a programmer. Cuba, a graduate of California Institute of the Arts (CalArts), film and animation programs, had initially contacted Whitney to discuss issues of Computer Art. "Whitney was one of the few people who was doing computer animation from the point of view of an artist," Cuba said. When Whitney had made it possible for students at CalArts to work at the Jet Propulsion Lab, Cuba took advantage of the opportunity. He got an account and began computer animation on the equipment. Cuba was the first student from CalArts to create a computer animation. Cuba worked with Whitney for a year before taking a job at Robert Abel and Associates, as a member of the technical support team.

The introduction of the Internet in the late 1960s created a means for wide-range computer networking. During that time, a student named Ed Catmull started at the University of Utah. A former Boeing employee, Catmull had received his degree in physics. At the university, Catmull enrolled in a computer graphics course taught by Ivan Sutherland. Sutherland began teaching at the university in 1967 after the he was recruited by David Evans, a computer scientist and head of the school's then new computer science program. Catmull was interested in computer graphics as an alternative to creating hand-drawn animation. The research led by Evans and Sutherland created international attention for the university's computer science program. In 1968, Sutherland built one of the first Virtual Reality systems that used a Head Mount Display with individual monitors for each eye and a position tracker that enables a computer to update the views based upon where the subject is working. That year, David Evans founded Evans and Sutherland—a Utah based company in the business of creating flight simulators that incorporate interactive computer generated displays of the various environments. (Rosebush 1994)

Schools continued to include aspects of computer graphics. In 1967, Donald Greenberg included computers in the School of Architecture at Cornell University, and MIT's Gyorgy Kepes founded the Center for Advanced Visual Studies. Apart from MIT, and University of Utah several computer science research labs were created at universities in the 1960s. Such examples include the University of Pennsylvania that began a Ph.D. program in computer science, Brooklyn Polytechnic's Computer Animation Department, Stanford University's Stanford Research Institute, and Purdue University's Computer Science Department.

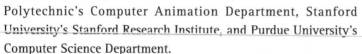

Scanimate is an analog animation computer used to create animated visual effects during the 1970s

By 1969 the blueprints were drawn for an analog computer system called the Scanimate. The creation of Lee Harrison III, this device was an improved version of the ANIMAC created in 1962. The Scanimate allowed the artist to create animation through the use of analog circuitry. Unable to create through keyboard commands, the user connected wires to patch boards and adjusted knobs, literally wiring each animation together. Like most of the computer equipment in the early days, it took a mix of technicians and artists that understood the subtleties of color and motion to create an image on the Scanimate. Today, most computer images are produced through digital frame buffers, or in large RAM-based memory arrays. In the early days of the Scanimate, the CRT could be considered the analog "memory" of the system, with the scan manipulations being addressed as offsets to the information "stored" in memory. The big difference was that the information was actually represented optically, so the animators could defocus the re-scan camera, place diffusion, refraction, reflection, or star filters between the camera and the CRT.

Once the images were scanned through a progressive scan monochrome camera, the animator could create real-time animation effects. A series of ramp, sine/cosine generators, bias and gain potentiometers and multipliers and summing amplifiers would be patched together to produce an animated sequence on the cathode-ray tube (CRT). A single sequence button would start the animation either manually or on cue from a Society of Motion Picture and Television Engineers (SMPTE) time code from videotape. As the animation ran, the hundreds of knobs could be adjusted, resulting in immediate modifications of the end product. The animator would run the animation several times while tweaking various parameters towards a desired behavior. The most famous Scanimate-generated film sequence was the brief color image of the *Death Star* as it emerged from behind a planet in the first *Star Wars* film. In 1972, Harrison III and Ed Tajchman won an Emmy from the Academy of Motion Pictures and Sciences for their work with Scanimates.

By the end of the 1960s, A. Michael Noll held several patents in the area of computer technology. From the time he was introduced to computers in 1962, he knew that he wanted to advance the medium's uses in the arts. He progressed to researching interactive methods of the computer and created a 3-D input device. The computer and 3-D joystick connected to a scan display with a buffer of memory. This formed the basis for the first television raster scan connected to a computer. He created the first 3-D computer-generated ballet and went on to create a device called the feelie device or tactile communication that allowed the user to receive force feedback from a 3-D computer-generated object through sensory motors connected to a Joystick. The patent granted in the early 1970s, "Was broad enough to include all present day virtual reality. The basic idea of a computer, 3-D display, 3-D input, and force feed back coming back to you, that's what the patent covered," Noll said. Though Noll's device lacked the gloves and the half-mirrored head mount display commonly used for virtual reality today, the underlying concepts and objectives are the same. "My objective was to interest other people—artist, choreographer, others and have them now pick this up as a tool and then use it. I am not an artist; it wasn't for me to do that. I just wanted to do things crudely and well enough to excite and interest others who would be better at it than me." Noll published his findings in various fine arts and technology journals. Noll left Bell Labs in 1972.

Rapid developments in computer technology continued along with video technology in the 1970s. New hardware was introduced during this decade as well. Memorable technology introduced in this decade included the Imax film format by Canadians Robert Kerr, Roman Kroiter, and Graeme Ferguson (1970). In the video arena, the U-matic 3/4" videotape was introduced in 1971. Nam June Paik and Shua Able assembled a video synthesizer with colorizer, keyer oscillators, and a mixer. The concept of non-linear editing was on the horizon in the early 1970s after the CMX 300, a computerized videotape editing system was introduced for on-line editing. Digital Video Time Based Correctors and digital audio were also products of the early 1970s. The Digital Video Effects devices introduced in the late 1970s made it possible to create various effects using scale and translated into moving video, capturing freeze frames and leaving trails. The laser videodisc was introduced in 1978 and made commercially available.

As the cost of computer memory went down, it became possible to produce raster displays at an affordable price. Raster displays required one bit of memory for every pixel represented on the screen. In the early days, a bit of memory was a dollar, so to achieve the basic 500 x 500 line image suitable for TV it required 250,000 points. In addition, 4 bits per point or 1 million bits was necessary to create reasonable color. 1 million bits cost $1 million dollars. The only people who could afford that level of memory were the military. Over the years, the price of memory went down to a fraction of that cost and was available for a penny per bit. This resulted in more available color displays that enticed more artists to create images using this digital technology.

The legacy to produce faster and cheaper computer systems continued in 1971 with the introduction of the microprocessor, a small computer chip that allowed for the start of microcomputers or personal workstations. The microcomputer era made it possible for video games to be available to the general public, thus fostering the rapid development of interactive programming.

Atari, founded in 1972 by Nolan Bushnell, was one of the first companies to focus on the development of interactive video games. The company hit the video game industry with "Pong", its first video game release. In 1975, the personal computer industry was on the rise with the advent of Paul Allen and Bill Gates' product, the Altair 8800 computer kit. The kit became "the first affordable useful computer an average person can buy and costs $500 with 256 bytes of RAM" (Rosebush 1994). Paul Allen and Bill Gates wrote a BASIC interpreter to run on the kit and founded Microsoft. That year IBM introduced their 5100 personal desktop computer. In 1975, Seymour Cray constructed the Cray-1 the fastest supercomputer. This machine allowed for faster processing of graphics and rendering time.

Inventions of the mid-1970s included the design of Video Place, a device that allowed the participant to truly become "virtual" as they were able to see a computer-generated representation of themselves in a digital environment. In 1975, Steve Jobs and Steve Wozniak constructed the Apple II personal computer. The Apple cost $1,295 and came with a display monitor and 16 Kbytes of RAM and ROM. The speed of computer technology development could be measured by the Intel chip. In 1970, Intel introduced the 1 Kbit memory chip and by the end of the decade, the 64 Kbit memory chip became available.

In the 1970s, the University of Utah continued to make significant contributions to improving the quality of digital imaging. The development of the research center and organizations boosted the development of computer art imaging technologies. Institutional research centers such as the University of Utah represented think tanks for the development of imaging tools. *Smooth Shading 3-D* or *Gouraud Shader* (1971) was developed by Henri Gouraud at Utah; this program marked the beginning of the transition from vector to raster graphics. In 1974, Bui Toung-Phong developed a new shading method that was later called *Phong Shading*. The Phong shader was capable of representing smooth reflective surfaces. Ed Catmull working at the University of Utah created *Motion Picture Language* (1972) an animation language, and z buffer (1974) technique, which was detailed in his doctoral dissertation. The z buffer is a term used to describe the area of memory devoted to temporary storage of the depth data for the pixels in a 3-D image. Advanced developments in the area of 3-D graphics were made by Fred Parke who created the first speech-synchronized, computer-generated facial animation during the mid-1970s. Frank Crow developed anti-aliasing methods for edge smoothing of graphics. By the early to mid-1970s dialogues about the future of computer graphics began to include the predictions of virtual reality. It is around that time that the Utah teapot made its grand entrance into computer graphics history. In 1977, Jim Blinn created bump image and texture mapping.

The University of Utah had an international reputation that attracted some highly qualified students to the computer science program. The distinguished group of Ph.D. students and faculty, that today reads like a who's who of computer graphics, consisted of the following: Jim Clark who later founded Silicon Graphics, Netscape, and later Healtheon/WebMD; Ed Catmull who co-founded Pixar; John Warnock who later founded Adobe Systems; Alan Ashton who founded WordPerfect; and, Suhas Patil who founded Cirrus Logic, a chip development company. Faculty David Evans and Ivan Sutherland founded Evans & Sutherland, a company that produces professional hardware and software to create visual images for simulation, training, and engineering.

The universities and their research centers continued the research of computer graphics often expanding and perfecting the findings of industry. In 1970, Charles Csuri established the Computer Graphics Research Group at the Ohio State University. Like most of the private research facilities, CGRG also worked on government projects, but the group's main interest was in the area of computer graphics as an art medium. In the 1970s, the CGRG group developed such programs as GRASS, a user oriented real-time animation system, created in 1972 by Tom De Fanti; ANIMA, a 3-D real-time animation system, created by Csuri in 1975, ANIMA II, a 3-D color animation system in 1977; and, ANimating Things Through Space (ANTTS) created by Csuri in 1979. In that same year, Nicholas Negroponte formed The Architecture Machine, another specialized lab at MIT.

"Throughout the history of technology, the way of the day forces a way of thinking on everybody and one can become blind to any other way of thinking"
——A. Michael Noll

By the mid-1970s, a new research center at the New York Institute of Technology (NYIT) in Long Island New York, began to address computer program needs. Founded by millionaire Alexander Schure, one of the Institute's goals was to create a research facility for the advancement of computer graphics. After a trip to Utah's facility, Schure was fascinated and set out to create a research facility with similar goals and ordered one of every computer system that he saw at Utah. He was interested in animation and had already hired over 150 cel animators to work on his concept for a traditional animated feature film. In his quest to create a center of excellence in computer graphics, he began a search to hire the top researchers to work on the most up-to-date computers and devices. Catmull was hired as the first director of NYIT's Computer Graphics Lab, and he in turn recruited several of the top researchers. Together the group worked countless hours on the development of computer graphics tools. "Alex was an accidental visionary," said Alvy Ray Smith a graduate of Stanford University and former researcher at Xerox PARC (Palo Alto Research Center). At that time, Smith worked with researcher Dick Shoup at Xerox PARC. He wrote an HSV (hue, saturation, value) color transformer and put that into Dick Shoup's program, *SuperPaint* (1973). "Xerox PARC decided not to do color," Smith said. Smith then began to search for another facility where he could gain access to a more advanced frame buffer. He contacted the researchers at Utah in a failed attempt to gain access to their facility and frame buffer system. The researchers informed him about Alex Schure, who by that time had already ordered a frame buffer system. Smith joined NYIT and gained access to millions of dollars in computer equipment. "At NYIT we got all the money we asked for; we had the best machines in the world," Smith recalls. "He bought the first commercially available 8 bit frame buffer." He said that he wanted the facility to remain a leading facility for computer graphics research. The group of four researchers convinced him to purchase two more 8-bit frame buffers. The researchers combined them to form the world's first 24-bit frame buffer. These machines allowed Smith to perfect researcher and former colleague Dick Shoup's interactive paint system to form what became the first 24-bit full color paint program. This program was one of the first major tools to be pioneered at the new facility. Garland Stern created *Softcel*, an animation language that simulated ink, opaque, and composites of cel animation. Some of the other pioneers at NYIT included James Blinn, Ralph Guggenheim, David DiFrancesco, Tom Duff, Rebecca Allen, Paul Heckbert, and Jim Clark.

By the mid- to late-1970s, NYIT had become known as the leading computer graphics research facility and employed over 60 researchers, most of them are today considered pioneers in the computer graphics arena. Utah's diminished funds for computer graphics caused the center to lose a great number of its top researchers to the new computer graphics lab at NYIT. Schure's millions had become useful in sustaining a group of researchers who longed to work on films. "We wanted to make a move," Smith explained, "we started 20 years before *Toy Story* wanting to make the first feature-length movie using computers; we knew it was going to happen." After a screening of his major film animation production *Tubby the Tuba,* the group became convinced of their theory. "I remember very clearly sitting in the front row of the premiere and I went to sleep cause that's the only way I could escape it," Smith recounts. Schure's failed attempt to produce a successful animation movie caused some animators to begin to accept other job invitations. The computer graphics division at Lucasfilm's primary focus was to create digital effects for feature films. The pioneering efforts shifted to other facilities such as Cornell University's Computer Graphics Department and Lucasfilm's computer graphics division (est. 1979).

At the University of Chicago, professor Tom De Fanti, a Ph.D. graduate of Ohio State University, headed an organization, Association of Computing Machinery's Special Interest Group on Computer Graphics (SIGGRAPH), which held its first conference in 1973. This became the primary conference for computer graphics' practitioners. The organization's goal was similar to that of E.A.T., to gather scientists and artists interested in contributing to the development of computer graphics. Also in 1973, the First International Computer Film Festival was held in Olympia, Wash-

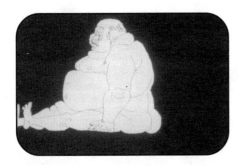

*Hunger,* an animated film by Peter Foldes. Image courtesy the National Film Board of Canada. This animation represented a pioneering effort in story-based 2D computer animation.

ington; this was one of the first computer animation film festivals. Other organizations of the 1970s included the New York National Computer Conference (NCC), which hosted an international computer art exhibition in the mid-1970s. In the late-1970s, programming languages such as C and UNIX were created at Bell Labs. In 1978, Bill Kovacs working at Robert Abel Associates developed an animation system. Kovacs, later went on to found Wavefront and transform the animation system into a commercial animation software package.

Both the art and the developing computer graphics findings were often published. A large number of magazines and journals were created in the 1970s. Prior to this, there were conflicts as to who invented what device first. Journals, publications, and early conferences provided artists and scientists alike with an effective forum for announcing new hardware, software, or style of imagery. By 1975, a new magazine, *Byte*, was created to address the issues relating to personal computers. In 1977, Computer Graphics World published its first magazine; today CGW is still focused on the digital imaging industry.

The technological developments of the 1970s facilitated a stream of milestone computer art and animated films. One of the most famous computer animation of the 1970s was the Academy

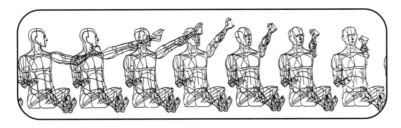

Plotter drawing created by William Fetter, 1962

Award nominated short, *Hunger* (Canada, 1974), directed by Peter Foldés. The film arguably contained the most unappealing characters of all 1970s animated films, but was a major milestone in the history of computer graphics and animation. To the film's credit, *Hunger* was one of the first computer animation to focus on a story rather than on technical capabilities.

In 1975, a young artist named David Em began work at the California Institute of Technology's Jet Propulsion Laboratory

(JPL), after a short stay at Xerox PARC where he was introduced to SuperPaint. Formally educated as a painter at the Pennsylvania Academy of the Fine arts in early 1970s, Em initially became interested in computer graphics after several experiments with analog video. He enjoyed working with the interactive paint system at Xerox PARC. At JPL, Em had the rare opportunity to be one of the few artists to work among pioneering scientists; however, it took him three frustrating years to develop the tools necessary to create his images. When Blinn was subsequently hired and implemented his own ideas, it made it possible for Em to create his fine arts images.

Voyager 2 Just After Ring Crossing. Courtesy JPL

At JPL, James Blinn and his team of artists and scientists created one of the most popular 3-D animation of that time, *Voyager 2*. The animation employed such techniques as bump and texture mapping to visualize the Voyager spaceship.

The 1980s saw the introduction of more technologies and techniques for creating fine arts with the computer. Several programs at various institutions allowed the artist and scientist to research growing areas of interest such as digital special effects, video art, and virtual reality. The early-1980s formation of Lucasfilm digital division solidified the computer as a commercially viable art tool. More and more artists and scientists once dedicated to the creation of art were making the transition to commercial art and effects. Tom Brigham, a programmer at NYIT, invented the technique known as raster morphing in 1982. In 1983, a computer artist named Manfred Mohr immigrated to America after a successful career as a computer artist in Paris dating back to 1968. Among other reasons, Mohr moved to America in search of accessible computing facilities. Hardware such as the IBM PC, introduced in 1980, and the Apple II of 1984, continued the push to make computers more accessible to the general public. The companies continued to compete with each other for a share of the consumer market.

Digital image created by Joel Slayton at MIT, 1981. 20 x 24 Polaroid

"When artist and engineers work together, the result is something neither can expect."
– Billy Klüver

Manfred Mohr: Approach to Creating Art

At a time when most computer artists were interested in recreating some aspect of their environment through two and 3-D computer programs, Manfred Mohr was on a path to creating abstractions. The South Germany born artist began his formal art career at the Design University. It was there that Mohr was

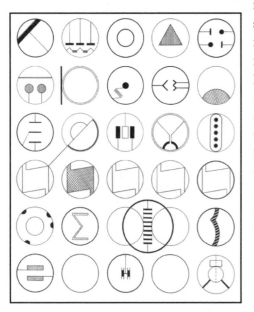

*Zeichnung* created by Manfred Mohr, 1967 ink on paper

introduced to avant-garde art. After receiving a scholarship in 1961 from the City of Pforzhim, he intended to continue art school in Barcelona. Mohr moved to Barcelona but never attended any courses. Instead, he spent two years as a musician touring Spain. In 1963, he made another attempt at school and enrolled in the Ecole des Beaux-Arts in Paris where he won a prize for his lithography in 1965. Mohr became interested in the computer in 1966 when he began noticing the IBM computers in the city of Paris. But Mohr did not know how to use the computer or more importantly how it could be utilized to create art. It was only in 1968 when he attended a lecture by French composer Pierre Barbaub, a musician who was the first to use computer programming to compose music that Mohr was truly sold on the medium. "We became good friends" Mohr says, "We set up a course for programming because we did not know what we were doing at the time. A group of us got together." The group, made up of artists, philosophers, and scientists was formally called the Art et Informatique and held meetings at the Université de Vincennes in Paris. The University later received a corporate donation of a PDP, its first computer. PDP also assisted the group with basic instruction on how to write a program on the system. Mohr bought a book on programming and began to teach himself.

Desperate to output his work to a plotter, Mohr soon broke away from the group and began using the facilities at the Meteorology Institute in Paris. "I saw on television that the Meteorology Institute had one of the first plotters at the time to draw weather maps." Mohr requested permission to work at the Institute. He wrote a letter to the institute explaining the importance of the facilities to his studies at the university. For the next twelve years, Mohr worked at the Institute at night. In describing the facilities at the institute Mohr says, "I had access to a large flatbed plotter, 4 x 5' and a computer. At that time, no one was doing anything like this so they were all curious. My other friends at the university in Paris were not allowed to work there so they had to look elsewhere. None of them ever found such a beautiful set up." A few years later, the Methodology Institute received other new plotters. Mohr now had a plotter to himself. In 1968, Mohr had the first one-man computer art exhibition in Europe.

"My art is not mathematical but is a statement shaped out of my experience. I am not trying to illustrate cold mathematics, but a vital philosophy," says Mohr, a former printmaker. Prior to using the computer, Mohr had been interested in informal action painting that was based on improvisation. "I become more interested in deciding something before hand, that I have a program set up before I begin to create something." The computer offered him the opportunity to start writing programs to decide the image through the algorithm. "That's why I got into geometry, I could write a program to calculate the geom-

P-49 Formal Language create by Manfred Mohr, 1970 ink on paper

etry." Mohr admits that he was not interested in creating 3-D images on the computer. "The most I did was kind of a relief drawing. I am more interested in the graphic aspect of something, I am interested in the semiotics, I am interested in a sign. The flatness of a drawing houses a certain ambiguity as to what it is and you destroy this ambiguity when it becomes 3-D. I am not really interested in showing the reality of something. The drawing doesn't have to prove itself. The ambiguity of something is very important to me."

In 1972, Mohr advanced his line computer automated drawings to another level. "I started working with cubes cutting up cubes to derange the symmetry to create new constellations of interest. I like to invent a rule that may be scientific but not show the rule but the results of it." Mohr views the computer as a "aesthetic filter." He explains, "the computer must pass through my ideas to come out as my ideas. I use the computer to really get into my work. I am locked in a figurative world. I am an absolute abstract thinker and I don't want to interpret the world but I want to invent a world. My questions are almost never visual, they are curiosity. Like what happens if I cut a cube in four and turn the four randomly without adding a visual solution for them. I must calculate and draw to see. I could only get my visuals after a concentration of programs that show how to do something and then develop it. After I say ahah I could have done this by hand but I didn't." The computer guides Mohr to the possibilities of the geometric art shape. These would have been impossible to visualize in any other medium.

The Meteorology Institute changed locations, and in 1983 Mohr moved to New York City in search of access to other advanced computer facilities. America offered Mohr the opportunity to get reasonably priced computers. He purchased a PDP 11/23, one of the first microcomputers. "It was a big machine, and I had a plotter which I got from a company called Alpha Merix, its like the stars came falling from the sky." Mohr offered his services to the company in return for a complementary plotter and for years he worked from his studio as a pre-

P-197-H created by Manfred Mohr, 1977-79 ink on paper

tester for the company's plotter. Mohr had indeed found ways to gain the access and equipment necessary to continue his art.

Programmers and artists continued to write proprietary software programs to facilitate the creation of art. Up to mid-1980, there were few commercially available software programs available for creating art. Programs such as Z-GRASS written by De Fanti and used by such video artists as Jane Veeder and Copper Giloth are testament to the continued collaboration among artists and computer scientists in the early 1980s. By 1983, an abundance of commercial hardware and software began to surface. The Quantel Paintbox is a commercial system that was introduced to expand the possibilities of video production. The system allowed the artist to paint directly onto video among other things. In 1984, Cubicomp introduced a commercial animation package for the IBM PC platform. That year, Wavefront software company introduced their interactive real-time commercial animation software that runs on the Silicon Graphics Iris workstation.

The production of computer art continued to be facilitated by both scientist and traditional fine artist. The success of the artistic value in the art was measured in technological sophistication rather than content and aesthetic merits. In 1986, Kenneth Knowlton in an invited statement for the SIGGRAPH art show catalog wrote: "We are not yet beyond the gee-whiz stage of cuteness, stunts, and novelty for its own sake." The former Bell Labs researcher recommended that artists and scientists embark upon a path that concentrates on improving the current computer tools" (SIGGRAPH Catalog, 1986). At this point," he wrote, "it does not make much sense to me to be trying to produce better computer art. The more appropriate challenge is to create better environments for the development of art-making tools." By the end of the 1980s, the computer interface's ability to facilitate the creation of high-end art and animation was evident.

*Luxo Jr.* a 2 minute short animation created by Pixar Animation Studios in 1986 and was nominated for an Academy Award for Best Animated Short

Quality products from commercial animation companies such as Pacific Data Images' *Waldo C. Graphics,* a motion capture

*Tin Toy* created by Pixar Animation Studio won the 1988 Academy Award for Best Animated Short

character, and Pixar's *Tin Toy* (1988) is a milestone project that marked the results of decades of development of technology and the aesthetics of computer graphics. *Tin Toy* is the first computer animation to win an Academy Award for Best Animated Short. Other inspiring works include PDI's *Locomotion* and *Burning Love* both of 1988, and *Knick Knack* (1989).

## Conclusion

Though a host of artists continued to work in the computer medium in the 1990s, major milestones in the area of non-commercial animation and graphics were few and far between. The final major milestone for non-commercial computer imagery came in 1997 with the creation of *Bunny,* a film by Blue Sky Studios. Written and directed by Chris Wedge, the film won the Academy Award for Best Animated Short Film in 1998. The next memorable award came in 2002 when Pixar's *For the Birds* won the Academy Award for Best Animated Short. But creating fine arts with the computer was not as popular as creating commercials or digital movie effects. A great number of the computer artists today seek employment in the digital movie effects industry, while a small group of others continue the battle to gain acceptance and the respect of fine artists in the art galleries in across the world.

The next chapter looks at the development of commercially driven computer graphics and its use in movie making and television production.

# Chapter 5
# Digital Movie Effects

A Brief History

Created in 1968, the film *Space Odyssey 2001* became the first feature film to incorporate the use of computer graphics visuals. It became the exemplar for the future of digital visual effects. This film was only the beginning of what would become a major turning point from experimental animation to commercially applicable digital effects. By 1970, William Fetter, a researcher at Boeing, created perhaps the first television commercial to use 3-D models. The 30-second commercial demonstrated the use of the Norelco razor. The computer generated vector graphics animation included lip sync and prospective (Rosebush 1994).

During this time, various companies began to address the desire for computer graphics in commercial projects and feature films. After gaining production experience at Evans and Sutherland and partner company, Information International Incorporated (I.I.I. or Triple I), John Whitney, Jr. and colleague Gary Demos formed the Motion Picture Production Group in 1974. The two then used computer graphics in the film *Westworld*, the first feature to use full screen raster graphics. The group did several television commercials for USA and the European markets and also created the effects for movies such as *The Looker* (1981).

In 1976, a London-based company called System Simulator Ltd. created a Computer-Generated Image (CGI) sequence for the movie *Alien*. By creating a program that generated random wire-frame mountains, the company was able to avoid the complex task of building an entire terrain of mountains. This was a cost-effective means of solving the problem as it would have required a huge database to create this simulation using conventional CGI techniques. With limited computer processing unit (CPU) power, the CGI artist often came up with clever means of compensating for the limitations of the computers. One of the first studios in New York to address the commercial demands for digital effects was a company called Digital Effects (1977) led by Judson Rosebush, Jeffrey Kleiser, and Donald Leich.

George Lucas founded Lucasfilm in 1971 and began creating his first film around that time. By 1973, he released *American Graffiti,* which was nominated for an Academy Award. The film introduced the concept of multiple story lines and secured Lucas a place in the history of filmmaking. In 1974, he began working on the concept and design of *Star Wars*, a film that ultimately combined traditional special effects and digital effects. Lucas then established Industrial Light and Magic for the production of traditional special effects and Skywalker Sound to edit and mix sound tracks for *Star Wars* in 1975. In 1977, Lucasfilm's *Star Wars* employed the use of digital visual effects created by Larry Cuba. "A couple of students from CalArts had gotten involved with the *Star Wars* project," Cuba said. "They had mentioned to me that there was someone on the crew that was looking for some computer animation. All the effects for the first *Star Wars* movie were done with models, miniatures, and traditional special effects photography. There was one scene that was supposed to be a computer readout. They were looking to see if this could be done with computer animation." At the time there were only a few people that Lucas could turn to for computer graphics. This included such companies as MAGI and Triple I. Cuba bid on the project as a freelancer and won.

*Star Wars* opened in 1977 and became the largest grossing film to that date. The success of *Star Wars* prompted Lucas to experiment more with computer-generated imagery in his next feature. He had plans to create a realistic digital scene in his next movie *The Empire Strikes Back* and began talks with the animation house Triple I. The plans were to create a sequence where realistic computer-generated fighter planes fly in formation. He contracted the computer animators at Triple I to create the animation. The finished animation, however, was not included in the final cut.

In the late 1970s, Robert Abel and Associates, a motion

graphics house, began using computers as an independent tool for creating commercials. In 1979, John Hughes and others at Robert Abel and Associates designed an animation simulation for Disney's *The Black Hole.*

In 1979, after five years at the New York Institute of Technology, Ed Catmull went to work for Lucasfilm as the head of the computer graphics division. Lucasfilms had a promising future and was interested in using computer-generated images for the purpose of movie making. With Catmull as vice president, the new division was well on its way to becoming one of the premiere companies for the production of commercial effects. "We were primed for George Lucas's call when it came," said Alvy Ray Smith who also left NYIT to work at Lucasfilm. Catmull recalls: "In 1979, I left and started the research lab at Lucasfilm. There I found what was missing at NYIT: a sense of story" (Catmull 1998). Smith supported Catmull as head of computer graphics. Smith explains, "Lucas was another accidental visionary. He wanted to modernize the film industry whose technology was stuck back in the 1940s. He knew that computers could be used to modernize the machinery and, we mistakenly thought that he understood that you can use computer technology to modernize the content as well. But after I was there for a couple of weeks I realized that he didn't get that part of it. He hired us to build three new machines: a digital video editor, a digital audio synthesizer, and a digital optical paint program (eventually named Pixar)."

Though the researchers had the expertise to build the equipment, it was not what they expected. "We assumed that what he was really up to was that he wanted his hands on the hottest graphics talent in the world so he could use them in his film, but that's where we were wrong. He didn't know about that. We put together the best computer graphics team in the business. It was somewhere around then when I realized that George didn't know what to do with us. George never did come and ask us to be in the movies. But Paramount did. Paramount came in to use Industrial Light and Magic (ILM). They hired ILM to create special effects for the movie *Star Treck II.* The director wanted some computer graphics in the film," Smith explained. The people at ILM then pointed the director to the computer graphics division. This encounter with Paramount allowed the computer graphics team to work on a 60-second scene for the movie. After a series of discussions with the director, Smith agreed to draw up the storyboard to show the director what could be possible with the equipment. Smith recalls: "That night was the most exciting night of my life because I knew that I had a shot at the big time. Nobody ever gets to design sixty seconds of a major motion picture. Usually they come to you and assign you the job, but here they had asked me to tell them what to put in the movie." Smith drew up the storyboard that deliberately included all the computer graphics research specialties of the employees at the computer graphics division, such as particle systems, and fractal mountains. Even more importantly, the project provided an opportunity for the division to show Lucas what the group was capable of doing. "A sixty-second commercial to George is what this really was," said Smith. Smith knew just how to get Lucas's attention. "I had watched George long enough to know that he was always aware of the camera; he could maintain a distance and focus on the cameraman's decisions." Knowing this fact about George, Smith and researcher Loren Carpenter designed an elaborate camera shot that was impossible to achieve through conventional camera techniques. "From then on he put us into his next movie."

"The advent of Lucasfilm's computer graphics division is viewed by many as a major milestone in the history of computer graphics. Here the researchers had access to funds, but at the same time they were working under a serious movie maker with real, definite, goals" (Morrison 1994). The group made up of several researchers from the NYIT Computer Graphics Lab had not been used to such time pressure, but were determined to make films.

The commercial application of computer graphics had commanded the attention of a much larger audience than that of its experimental animation and fine arts counterpart. Commercial animation advertised a product, goods, or services and was usually aired on television or through effects on the silver screen. Experimental animation shorts, such as *Vol Libre* created by Loren Carpenter in the late-1970s, were seldom seen on television and were often limited to computer graphics conferences such as SIGGRAPH. Although most commercial animation consisted of basic flying corporate computer generated logos, more and more artists became interested in creating commercial projects. Some of the labs creating commercial digital effects in the 1970s were Triple I, NYIT, Lucasfilm, Mathematical Applications Group Inc. (MAGI), Digital Effects, and Robert Abel and Associates.

With creations such as Atari's Grand Track, a racing simulation arcade video game which used a steering wheel and gas pedal to control a simulated car on a track in 1974 and Nintendo's home market variation of the Pong video game, and the advent of new game companies such as Activision, the gaming world was ready for establishing more home games in the 1980s. A large contribution to the gaining success in the home markets was the price of the hardware. In 1979, Atari 400 and 800 personal computers cost less than $1,000, and with the introduction of color raster display in 1977, consumers were able to take advantage of color game monitors. By 1981, the home video industry had already become a billion-dollar industry. The market saw the introduction of Infocom's *Zork*, a personal computer version of an adventure game, Namco's *Pac Man*, an arcade game, and *Donkey Kong* with the character Mario. Atari introduced the DataGlove, which allowed users to interact within a 3-D computer graphics world, much like virtual reality. By the late 1980s, Nintendo introduced the Game Boy, a hand-held video game with stereo sound and interchangeable game cartridges.

Several major computer animation studios were created in the early 1980s. Stanford educated engineer Carl Rosendahl founded Pacific Data Images (PDI) in 1980. Today, PDI is considered the oldest computer graphics company in existence. Charles Csuri of the Ohio State University and investor Robert Kanuth of The Cranston Companies cofounded the Ohio-based computer graphics company Cranston/Csuri Productions (CCP) in 1981. The company produced over 700 animation spots for over 400 clients, but went out of business after 7 years. In 1981, Digital Productions was founded by Gary Demos and John Whitney, Jr. of the former Triple I. The studio went on to create several popular digital effects spots including work on the feature film *The Last Starfighter* (1985).

In 1982, computer graphics found its way into yet another feature film, *Tron*. The film used the most computer graphics created sequences to that date and was the first film to replace what would have been done with traditional effects media. Triple I, Abel, MAGI, and Digital Effects created the visual effects for the movie. The $20 million budget film produced by Disney Productions employed some of the top computer graphics firms to produce over 20 minutes of computer animation. The film used both raster and vector graphics techniques as well as photo-rotoscoping, masking, and coloring through multiple camera passes. Richard Taylor was hired as the visual effects supervisor, and was mainly responsible for coordinating the effects from the various companies involved. His background as a film/lighting specialist and former director of both Abel and Triple I, made him the ideal person for supervising a film with various scenes of simulated light effects. Abel did the vector graphics for the opening title and within the animation. As they were not equipped to do raster graphics, that was handled by animators such as Chris Wedge of MAGI and others.

*Tron* did not receive an award for its visual effects. But the film was viewed as a major victory for the computer graphics field, though it had a negative impact on Hollywood's attitude toward computer graphics. This made it challenging for other studios to locate the funding to create 3-D feature animated films.

In 1982, after *Tron* was completed, Taylor opened a west coast branch of MAGI. There Taylor created commercials, including the first commercial to be awarded a Clio Award for computer simulation and for *Worms War 1* for an Atari video game of the same name. The category for computer animation began in 1983. Taylor went on to direct computer animation and live action commercials for ad campaigns for 7Up and Duracell.

By 1983, the Lucasfilm's Computer Division created Pixar, a computer system which was used to produce computer animation shorts. Alvy Ray Smith, Bill Reeves, and Disney trained traditional animator John Lasseter created an animation short, *The*

*Adventures of Andre and Wally B* (1984), that incorporated the Disney principles of animation. The two-minute animation short showed a Disney still character with large expressive eyes and a bee that he tries to outwit. The character animation was staged in the foreground of a well-rendered background of 3-D computer-generated trees. Though the main character's motion was not perfect, it was one of the best character animation created to that date, and its simplistic sphere-based design allowed for little compromise in the motion. Unlike many classically trained animators at that time, Lasseter, a top graduate of the California Institute of the Arts, believed in the computer and its potential to create animation. "He was willing to listen to the computer people," Smith said, "his generosity was to show that he was ready to tolerate the computer."

Lucas did not make any efforts to market the systems developed by the computer graphics division. "He didn't get the basic concept that everyone in Silicon Valley has," Smith says, "that is once you build a prototype, that is when you pour capital on it and turn it into a product." Smith then went to speak with Catmull, the head of the computer division, with the idea of forming a company. He reasoned with Catmull that: "George didn't know what to do with us and I believe he is going to fire us. It would be a sin to let this world class team disperse." Both men went out to a bookstore that day and bought books on how to start a company. Steve Jobs, chairman of Apple Computer, wanted to buy the company and become CEO. The researchers disagreed and Jobs finally agreed to provide the venture capital for the new company.

In 1986, the Computer Graphics Division broke free of Lucasfilm with a $10 million purchase by Steve Jobs. Before leaving, Catmull hired Doug Kay and George Joblove to continue the Computer Graphics Division for ILM, as Lucas still wanted to have computer graphics capabilities. President Ed Catmull and Vice President Alvy Ray Smith headed up the new animation company called Pixar. "We started off as a hardware company building Pixar image computers," Smith said. "We had built the prototype for George, so then we started selling the machine. It was a great machine but we didn't have marketing skills honed enough to teach people what it was. The only company that got it was Disney."

In 1986, Smith got the green light on an 18-month negotiation with Disney to build the Computer Aided Production System (CAPS). The CAPS was computer hardware and software, which allowed the company to create digital cel animation. The only part of the traditional animation process that was maintained was the drawing of the cels, after which they were input into the computer. The system allowed the animators more control over the animation process. With CAPS Smith said, "the quality shot way up, they had better quality than they had ever had before in the animation business. They could do a multiplane spot in every shot. They could have 30 to 100 levels in their multiplane shots instead of five." The change to CAPS was evident in all Disney movies that followed, including *Rescuers Down Under* and *The Great Mouse Detective*. Pixar delivered the systems cheaper and faster than outlined in the contract with Disney. This was the cornerstone for a successful relationship built on mutual respect, and that led to collaborations on future fully computer animated feature films. In that year, Pixar produced *Luxo, Jr.,* a character animation short about the relationship between a father and son table lamp. The company created several award-winning animation shorts, but continued to focus on the commercially viable aspects of feature films and commercials. Pixar, however, made no profit in its first five years of operation.

In 1986, Robert Abel and Associates was purchased by Omnibus Computer Graphics who also purchased Digital Productions. The two cofounders of Digital Production, John Whitney, Jr. and Gary Demos, left and formed Whitney Demos Productions, which later became Demos Production. In 1987, Omnibus went out of business. The breakup of Robert Abel and Associates gave rise to such companies as Rhythm & Hues, Metrolight, and Kleiser-Walczak Construction Company, and fueled other existing companies such as PDI, Lucasfilm, Boss Films, and many others. Demos Production led by Whitney and Demos split up to form two independent companies, U.S. Animation Labs, led by Whitney, and DemoGraphics formed by Demos.

John Hughes, President of Rhythm and Hues, reflected on the founding of the company in 1987. Hughes had worked at Abel for 10 years. "Randy Roberts, one of the top directors at Abel and Associates came to me and suggested that we form our own company. I was not happy with the direction Robert Abel and Associates was going, consolidating with Digital Productions, because the leadership of the company of Omnibus, Digital Productions, and Robert Abel and Associates had made the decision that the future lie in the Cray computer. At Robert Abel and Associates, we were running UNIX on workstations and we thought that the future was going to be UNIX workstations with many computers rather than relying on a single massive processor like the Cray. There were huge technical and political battles being fought between the digital production people who insisted that multiple smaller computers could never rival what could be done with a single Cray computer."

The fact that Omnibus had purchased Robert Abel and Associates meant that the company would be grouped together with Digital Productions to function in a predominantly Cray computing environment. "So, there was this intense revelry in what we thought was a huge technical mistake," Hughes said. The time was right for Hughes to branch off to a new company. "So Randy came to me and said 'let's start our own company, it will be you and I,' I said fine." The company was to be headed by Hughes in production, and Randy Roberts as director. After the founding group was formed, Roberts backed out of the plans to pursue a career in live-action film directing. The group went on to form Rhythm and Hues in 1987. Hughes had planned to run the company from his studio with his Silicon Graphics workstation. New Years Eve, a fire in the studio close to Hughes' resulted in damage to his computer. As part of the insurance settlement, Hughes was given a new SGI workstation. The start-up company used this computer, and others, along with Wavefront software to create their first job in April 1987. Today, the company has 250 employees.

Computer generated character animation that incorporates Disney's principles of traditional animation are now frequently incorporated in commercial spots and shorts. These 12 principles of animation are established rules created by Walt Disney Company to govern the behavior of 2-D traditional animation. When these principles are applied to a 3-D computer animation character, the 3-D character is referred to as character animation. Commercials such as the *Snacky* by Pacific Data Images of the late 1980s were some of the early computer-generated character animation. The animation, created for a Japanese company, reflected advancements in the technology. Computer characters used in these early commercials were appealing to viewers. They were like 3-D computer version of Walt Disney's cel characters that the audiences had already become familiar with. Few animated shorts made any serious attempts to animate a realistic computer-generated human. By focusing on clever facial expressions and human-like movements of the character, they were able to create less complicated but equally effective character animation.

Digital effects in feature films began to truly push the boundaries of the computer graphics medium. Morphing and other visual effects techniques were incorporated to form, more so that ever before, seamless effects. Effects houses, such as Industrial Light and Magic worked on the production of over 30 feature films in the 1980s, most of which employed the use of digital effects. By 1989, such features as James Cameron's *The Abyss* was testament to the perfection of the craft. This academy award winning film proved that digital effects, as created by ILM, can be seamlessly composited with live action.

In the 1980s, computer graphics also found its way into other commercially viable areas. By the mid-1980s, computers became useful in various areas of simulation of real-life occurrences. One of the areas is forensics, which employs computer graphics to illustrate accidents and simplify medical cases in a courtroom. More recently, forensic animation was used by the prosecuting attorney in the O.J. Simpson trial.

The technology continued to develop throughout the 1980s. Most innovations were focused on improving the quality of this new medium for use in the commercial world. Silicon Graphics was founded in 1982 and created its first computer, the Iris, in

1984. The system was one of the fastest on the market to date and is capable of creating real-time vector graphics. By 1985, Wavefront and Alias were the primary off-the-shelf software packages available for the Iris. The Quantel Paintbox system was one of the first off-the-shelf video paint programs, and later, Quantel Harry for compositing digital video. In the area of analog video, Betacam SP replaced the video standards of Betacam and offered a much higher resolution, and Super VHS was an improved version of VHS, which was geared toward industrial users. Another concept, multimedia, was also formalized around this time. The first formal demonstration of this concept was done at SIGGRAPH. Multimedia uses the computer's CPU as a brain to control different internal or external devices, such as a video clip or sound file, to play externally or on the computer monitor. Avid's non-linear editing system, C++ appending, C programming, supporting object-oriented programming, and AT&T's Targa board for outputting video from the PC directly to videotape, were just some of the major technological innovations of the 1980s.

Attempts to create virtual humans continued to receive the attention at computer animation houses. In the 1990s, commercial artists focused on perfecting the tools of the trade. After years of development of the medium, the virtual human character was finally beginning to come out of the dark scenes usually created to hide the character's faults. The 1990s can be considered an era of feature film production that incorporated complex digital effects. *Terminator 2: Judgment Day* (1991), directed by James Cameron was this decade's first feature film with the most memorable digital effects. The film featured astounding digital effects created by ILM and PDI, using a combination of off-the-shelf and proprietary software. Computer graphics was used in the film to create a simulated liquid metal character. The technique of morphing was used extensively in the computer graphics' segments of the film, and a wire-removal process created at PDI, was used to erase the wire harness that supported the Terminator and motorcycle in a major jump sequence. The film was quite a success at the box office. PDI had proven that its proprietary image-processing software could produce amazingly flawless results.

Another successful film was Disney's *Beauty and the Beast*. This 1991 film also employed computer graphics to create a majestic ballroom where the 2-D hand-drawn characters danced. The digital ballroom blends seamlessly with the cel characters. Xaos, Inc. created the digital effects in the 1992 feature film *Lawnmower Man*. The feature, based on a virtual reality story, exhibited several spectacular fully computer graphics scenes. Around this time, Pixar signed an agreement with Disney to produce the first fully computer generated feature film. Within three years, the movie *Toy Story* (1995) was created at Pixar Animation Studio. Steven Spielberg's feature *Jurassic Park* (1993) showed the finest display of computer-generated creatures. The dinosaurs in the film were primarily the work of ILM's high-end computer graphics and Stan Winston's animatronics. The film represents a major milestone in the successful integration of all forms of effects tools.

Phil Tippett, an animator at ILM, developed a technique called go-motion that was used to animate the smooth movement of the bicycle sequence in *E.T. The Extra-Terrestrial*, in 1982. Go-motion made it possible for animators to photograph with motion blurs, creating the perception of smoother character motion on film. The technique was considered for *Jurassic Park*, but the computer team created more convincing results and won over the contract. This was a success for the animators using software programs such as Maya, Softimage, proprietary software, and the SGI platform, who were able to create more convincing results using CGI.

Steven Spielberg cofounded DreamWorks SKG (Spielberg, Katzenberg, Geffen) in 1995. The mid-1990s also represented a successful decade for computer-generated imagery in feature films. The most memorable features included *Twister* (1996); Spielberg's sequel *The Lost World: Jurassic Park* (1997); the epic *Titanic* (1997); one of the first computer animated films by DreamWorks' *Small Soldiers* (1998); PDI and DreamWorks SKG full computer animation feature *Antz* (1998); Pixar and Disney's second animated feature *A Bug's Life* (1998); DreamWorks SKG's animated biblical epic *The Prince of Egypt* (1998); and, the amazing acting of the mouse *Stuart Little* (1999).

Most of the animation shows still debut on the small screen. Television programming continues to control a large number of the animation created. Companies such as Colossal Pictures of northern California and Curious Pictures of New York are just two of the growing smaller companies that are creating computer animation for home viewers. Curious Pictures launched *A Little Curious,* a show that uses various styles of animation and premiered on HBO. Television became a stepping-stone for alternative animation to test the waters before flourishing into feature films. Such films as *Joe's Apartment, Rugrats, Bevis and Butt-head* (which was canceled from television because of its offensive content), and *South Park* are all examples of animated series that began on television and went on to become movie features. With productions such as Liquid Television, MTV has created a venue for alternative animation that are non-Disney-esque. This created an opportunity for others to join in on the creation of subcultural animation.

By the mid 1990s, Wavefront and Alias merged to form Alias/Wavefront and in 1998 introduced their signature product Maya, a high-end software package. The 1990s saw a surge of computer animation and the beginning of a new trend to create more full-length computer-animated features. Over 15 animated features were to be released in the years 1999 and 2000, of these, the majority incorporated significant forms of computer-generated imagery. Major studios such as Disney, Pixar, DreamWorks, SKG, Paramount, and Nickelodeon are at the forefront of this development. Pixar continues to team up with Disney and is working towards releasing a fully computer animated film every year. In 1999, the company released the sequel to *Toy Story, Toy Story II.*

## Conclusion

The future for digital effects and animation in feature films is very promising. The 2001 release of PDI/DreamWorks' *Shrek* reassured Hollywood's investors that 3-D computer animation was a new form of feature filmmaking. Earning over 62 million dollars in its opening weekend, *Shrek* proved that a string of successful 3-D features was more than a fairytale; it was the result of computer graphics with over 50 years of development. The film went on to win an Academy Award for Best Animated Feature Film in 2002. Other hyper-real computer animated features such as *Final Fantasy: The Spirits Within* 2001 did not do well at the box office, but was a monumental success for the 3-D animation area. 3-D features have earned their place in the filmmaking world. The release of Disney/*Pixar's Monsters, Inc.* and *Fox's Ice Age* both of 2001, once again shows the results of a well-written script and the versatility of the computer graphics medium. 2001 was the year the Academy of Motion Picture Arts approved a new category for the Oscars titled Best Animated Feature Film.

In 2002, Spider-Man was released and quickly earned the title of the first movie to gross over $200 million in 10 days. The CG team at Sony Pictures ImageWorks created 475 effects shots for the Colombia Pictures' film. Perhaps it also proved what can happen when seamless 3-D animation is integrated into a predictable live-action story line with big budget advertising efforts.

The long awaited DreamWorks film *Spirit: Stallion of the Cimarron* was released on Memorial day of 2002. The film seamlessly combined 2-D cel animation and 3-D computer animation to create a look similar to that of Disney's *Lion King.* This cycle has became all too common with animated feature films. Fully animated features that started back in the 1930s took on wings in the 1990s and have been flying high ever since with arguably little technical invention, and less deviation from the Disney storytelling norms. By perfecting the technology and polishing old stories, a safe and secure future lies ahead for the feature animation industry.

Ron Saks: Discovering A Passion

For every individual, discovering a passion for computer graphics will be different. The possibilities may be endless. Ron Saks had already discovered a passion for art and science before he began an academic career in computers that eventually lead to the path of computer graphics. In a time when computer graphics were not as flamboyant as they are now, and television and film did not embrace the medium as it does today, becoming a computer graphics practitioner did not promise the present salaries of the field.

After receiving a scholarship at the San Francisco Academy of Art, Saks, the former high school science major, decided to try to combine arts and science in college. At the Academy, he majored in fine arts, but his one session at the Academy would expire. He transferred to the University of California at Los Angeles, and joined the College of Letter and Sciences as an undeclared major. He later petitioned to join the Art Department of the College of Arts, in a process that eventually took a couple of years.

At the department, Saks took courses in drawing, painting, and photography, but it was in a foundation sculpture course that he began experimenting in time-based imagery. He considered himself a "2-D artist" and resisted a required sculpture course but eventually enrolled. One single assignment was given for the quarter. This assignment required the students to produce a sculptural piece that showed a process, and exploited the qualities of the cardboard material with which they were working. After thinking about the assignment for weeks, Saks eventually wound up building a large cardboard sculpture that had some match heads and a lens built into it with a specific focal length. He assembled it with a particular angle and took it outside on a bright, sunny day. The light of the sun was focused onto the match heads that lit them, and the cardboard sculpture set itself on fire. Pleased with the concept, Saks used slide photographs and 8-mm movie film to document the process of its deconstruction.

Saks presented the results as a documentation of the process. He knew that if the sculptural concept worked, he would not have any assignment to show to the professor; so, he wrote a paper describing the process, turned in the charred lens, and projected the images in the sculpture gallery. The motion picture film was projected on one side of the screen, and right next to it, the slide images that were static, being one-after-another

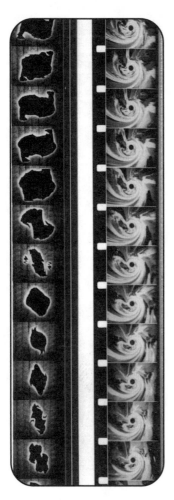

Film strips of images created by Ron Saks in 1977.

sequential images. The film showed the sculpture continuing to burn itself out and turn to ash, while on the other side the slide now showed the sculpture coming from the ashes and forming itself.

Through the sculpture project, Saks become interested in experiments that explored time and motion. He became excited in particular about art that changed over time and the way to record, display, and control those changes. His curiosity led him to enroll in animation courses at the University's Theatre Arts Department. There, Saks continued to focus on animation as a medium for dealing with art that changes over time.

As a graduate student of the Theatre Arts Department in the 1970s, Saks had little exposure to computers for experiments in computer animation. In fact, as an undergraduate student up until 1971, Saks did not have any experience using computers. He recalls that "unless you were a computer science major or engineer there really weren't any general computer literacy classes, and even in '71, '72, there weren't any microcomputers out there. You really didn't see micros until about '75." John Whitney, Sr. introduced Saks to computers in 1974. Whitney taught a course in the theories and concept of computer graphics at UCLA as a guest lecturer for one year.

Whitney was assisted by Larry Cuba who wrote a few algorithms specifically for the course. Saks recalls, "We'd go down to the biomedical lab where he had a computer that he could access. Larry would boot up the computer, and he'd show us the routines and some of the displays that we were getting." The course exposed Saks to different types of computer displays. "I was aware, at that point, of some of the different kinds of graphic applications, both in terms of motion control and computer-generated dot patterns—vector images that weren't displayed as lines but rather as points."

Having had a science background in high school and continuing to take calculus and physics in college, Saks was very interested in applied mathematics. As a graduate student, he found employment in the traditional animation effects field where he combined his knowledge of mathematics, animation, and computers. During the early-1970s, Saks began working as a cameraman at an educational animation company called Stephen Bosustow Productions. He was trained on how to use the camera, and was required to calculate the camera moves. "At times, these calculations were as simple as marking the camera moves with tick marks on masking tape or surgical rubber strips before shooting the moves on the cameras to the next position," he explained. Some cameras had counters. As a motor turned, the camera went up and down a column, or traveled east, west, north, and south while the counter changed values. On these counter-aided cameras, Saks had to figure out formulas for specific moves. There were various combinations of camera moves: "If you wanted to do a linear move, a slow-in, slow-out, or a curved move, you'd have to figure out some kind of formula...." Saks later got the opportunity to apply his computer knowledge when he began to plot the camera motion on a computer at his friend's place of work. While working at Stephen Bosustow Productions, he was also able to work on independent experimental films.

Saks became interested in the early computer graphic arts and artists in Los Angeles. He attended screenings where he viewed the works of computer graphics pioneers such as John Whitney's early work *Permutations*. He also saw *Odyssey 2001*, and was amazed by the motion control of the Stargate corridors sequence. These professional and private films intrigued him and inspired him to continue along the path of computer graphics.

Robert Abel and Associates began recruiting artists for their production environment and Saks, who was intrigued by the cutting-edge technology, was hired. "Abel was engaged in a very different technology—using this motion control technology to build some credible 3-D spaces. This technique was not common in conventional animation," Saks explained. Based on the success of commercial productions, Robert Abel began looking for practitioners to work at the company. Abel contacted Whitney and two others who had known Saks. Saks then contacted Abel concerning the available position and was hired in 1976.

The seasonal production industry allowed Saks the liberty to alternate between graduate school and work. Because of his background, Saks was hired as a cameraman and moved into technical directing. "I wasn't a programmer—there were some technical directors—I was a technical director more in art and compositing. There were some technical directors with more math and computer backgrounds." His duties on the job included camera work, designing the motions that were going to be done, devising strategies to execute those camera motions given the computer programs that were available at Abel, devising matte strategies, and compositing.

In 1979, Saks moved on and worked at various other companies but by this time, he had already worked with some of the principle effects practitioners and computer programmers in the Los Angeles area. A number of the practitioners from Abel and Associates went on to form companies of their own, while others became principle effects practitioners at major national companies. Saks worked at companies such as Astra Image Corporation-Paramount Studios, Pacific Title and Art Studios, Clara Vista Images, Rede Globo, Omnibus Productions and Abel-Graphix, before heading up Universal Studios computer animation department in 1985; at the same time he taught a course in computer animation at UCLA. He would later work for Cranston-Csuri Productions as the director of animation production, then as an animation instructor at The Ohio State University. Saks is currently a professor and department chair for film video and animation at the Columbus College of Art and Design, where he has worked as an associate professor since 1988.

# Chapter 6
# Advice on Training and Education

## Introduction

There are several ways you can prepare for a career in the computer graphics industry. You can receive a formal or informal education in preparation for this field. Formal education is an established academic program at a institute or university that usually leads to a degree or certificate of completion. An informal education is one where the individual is self-taught or learns through on-the-job training. In this section of schools, four main methods of schooling will be discussed: training at a institute, attending a university, the self-taught approach, and on-the-job training.

## Training At An Institute

One way to acquire training in the area of computer graphics is to attend a training institute. These institutes operate like a University's School of Continuing Education. The animation and multimedia classes usually focus on specific training in different software programs. They are good for anyone that is already in the industry or someone who is knowledgeable about the background and theories, or one who does not require much guidance. You can acquire some of the necessary training for becoming a computer graphics artist by attending these institutes. They are not accredited and you can attend as many classes as possible, and learn the different platforms that are necessary to advance in an area of emphasis.

## Attending a College or University

The college or university offers a formal education environment that leads to a degree in the general subject area. The university offers a more general approach to studying the field of computer graphics. Students must adhere to the courses outlined in the curriculum to receive the degree. These courses are usually broken down into various specialized areas. The University offers a supportive environment with the possibility of being taught by professionals from the industry and academics. If you choose this type of education, take advantage of this mix. Enroll in traditional fine arts courses and develop your traditional skills before becoming involved with the computer.

The college or university is the perfect place to experiment. Begin by studying the various aspects of computer graphics such as digital paint, modeling, lighting, and animation. Learn various types of animation and modeling software; do not limit yourself to being a specialist in a particular software program. "One of the largest issues," says Endla Burrows, Training Manager at ILM, "is that people who study computer graphics at the university tend to study a really narrow set of skills, or even a narrow set of software, and they don't get a full conceptual and artistic understanding of what they are trying to do. It is exceedingly frustrating to have someone come in claiming to be an animator because he or she knows the buttons on a particular software program. This is all about visual art."

Undergraduate students interested in this field should build a strong general fine arts foundation before zeroing in on an area of specialization. If a student becomes interested in animation, David Tart, an animator at Pixar, advises that he or she take various traditional animation courses and perhaps skip computer graphics altogether. They should take drawing, dance, acting, and any other course that places an emphasis on movement and timing in a real-life environment. Learn how to time works in a real-life environment before trying to simulate it in a computer environment. Jennifer Yu at the former PDI now PDI/DreamWorks finds that "people without a computer background can be really successful in an animation environment like PDI, but" she adds, "they need to develop confidence in approaching a computer." Those interested in modeling should take courses in sculpture, claymation, architecture, and any other class that forces you to examine and build 3-D objects. If you are interested in digital paint and image processing, you should take courses in painting, drawing, and photography. Learning the tradition methods of this new art form will only help strengthen the resulting digital image.

If you are enrolled at a university, you should focus on developing good problem-solving and creative skills for approaching computer effects. Though you probably won't have access to proprietary programs, you may, as Yu advises, try to create effects with whatever off-the-shelf software is available. Understanding the underlying principles is one of the most important components of the learning process. Newcomers to the field should produce as much as possible. Most university programs have realized the need for a solid theoretical foundation as well as practical training. Most programs are very individually oriented, where students produce their own animation. Though this is an excellent way for you to have hands-on experience in all forms of production, it does not prepare them for the teamwork environment of commercial production. It is important to have your own research, but it is also important to learn how to communicate and interact in a group situation by producing a collaborative project. Students learning at the university should also go out in the field and get some kind of practical training prior to finishing their degrees.

## The Self-Taught Approach

For most people, being self-taught is often not planned; rather, it is the result of access to tools, people, and resources. Today, there are so many different consumer grades of hardware and software on the market that getting your hands on a graphics package is not difficult. Even purchasing a computer and a couple of graphics packages is within the average person's means. In addition, there is an abundance of books, training materials, and websites to aid a beginner. But what is more challenging, is knowing how to prepare for the field as an artist. To become a computer graphics artist, understanding the aesthetics of the medium is paramount. If you do not have a traditional fine arts background, you must first start development in that area. Even the self-taught artist should take fundamental fine arts courses such as drawing, painting, and color theory. You may also choose to study reference books on these subjects; however, for the true novice, there is no substitute for learning the fundamentals under the guidance of an art teacher. This can be achieved through the continuing education department at a college. At this early stage, you can begin developing a visual vocabulary. Though visual literacy is built up over years rather than days, take time to really think about your message and the most appropriate visual composition through this new medium to create your art. Equip yourself with as many concepts and styles as possible. Keep a sketchbook and draw frequently. Speak with trained artists and allow them to critique your work. However, if you choose to do it, you must understand the elements that go into the composition of an image.

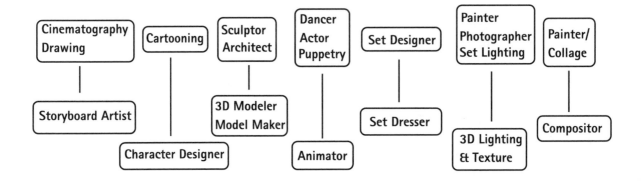

Traditional fine arts and design training prepares students for the animation industry. The chart above suggests some natural progression into an animation related career from a traditional beginning. The top boxes indicate the traditional careers and bottom boxes indicate a career in animation

One who has a fine arts background need only take their traditional art to the next level of the computer. The self-taught approach may first begin with a basic survey of the field. That is, learn as much as possible about the different career choices within the field. Speak to individuals who are doing what you wish to do before determining your area of emphasis; spend time at the library reading and researching the history and background of the field. Read the periodicals to get a feel for what is current. Most importantly, choose an area that best defines you. That may be answered by your response to these two questions: What do you like best about computer graphics? What type of fine arts do you do? For example, if you are a traditional fine arts painter, you may be interested in digital paint programs and texturing 3-D objects on the computer.

Do not allow the technology to determine what you should learn. You must use the technology to suits your needs. If you are traditionally a sculptor or in an area of fine arts or design that requires the building of 3-D objects, you may be interested in 3-D modeling on the computer. It is more important for animators to study traditional animation, rather than the details of particular software. "A lot of people have been trained to believe that if they know a software program then that makes them a character animator," Beth Sasseen, recruiting manager at ILM observes. "On one level they can claim to be technically proficient at something. Technically, meaning a digital technology, so it makes them technically savvy about something, but that kind of technical savvy, in terms of wanting to be a character animator, isn't enough to make them a character animator, but it probably isn't enough either to make them a technical director. They are sort of falling between a rock and a hard place," she explained. Sasseen warns that whether they are interested in technical directing or character animation careers, students need go beyond software training.

A self-taught approach can be used to acquire the skills beyond software training. You can acquire the skills for being a better artist by observing the works of experts in the arts. Sharon Calahan, lighting supervisor at Pixar took a self-taught approach to learning lighting. Over time, she learned by experimenting and trial and error with different lighting techniques. But she also learned by studying older films such as *Citizen Kane*. She explains, "I love jogging through it on my laser disc and watching the lighting, especially compositional lighting and the transitions between shots. It's just a very visually rich film. I like studying films like that and learning from them." Similarly, Stefen Fangmeier visual effects supervisor at ILM has taken a self-taught approach to prepare himself for a formally trained computer scientist as an artist.

### The Computer Purchase

Self-taught individuals sooner or later face the task of purchasing a computer. There are several philosophies for purchasing a computer. First, begin by being an informed consumer. Being informed

"It is always the danger that you get caught in technology and you lose your mind in technology because it is so fascinating. You always have to concentrate back to what you really want to do."
—Manfred Mohr

means that you should first know what you would like to do before you begin thinking about a computer purchase. Are you going to experiment with 2-D and 3-D software packages? What are you planning to accomplish with a new computer? The best advice is to buy the computer you can afford. Do not be overly anxious to get the latest top of the line system if your goal is to just get a feel for computer graphics. Today, the price of computer hardware and software is constantly declining. A consumer grade computer purchase today will be valued at half the price in the next year. If you are careful, you can take advantage of the market declines. Here is how: If your current goal is to learn a basic computer-drawing software, when researching a computer, buy one that can simply perform this task and not too much more. Get your feet wet. By the time you are ready to advance to a 3-D package, you can simply purchase more random access memory (RAM), and read-only memory (ROM) for your system and expand its capabilities. If you are already familiar with the computer and you are a fast learner, or if your goal is to create an animation, it may be wise to purchase a little more. But as a general note it is better to purchase in steps, purchasing as the need arises, and not purely from desire.

If your intention is to create fine arts images or any form of animation you should invest in a large monitor, at least 17 inches. The larger the monitor, the easier it is to work with in programs such as Photoshop, which tend to open several tools for easier access to the user. Consider two monitors rather than one big monitor. These can be linked together to make them act as one. This will allow you to have all your tools in view on one monitor and view your creation on another.

After you have purchased your computer, join various users' groups for hardware and software support. Experiment with different software programs and get a feel for the ones that are the most "user-friendly" and simple to use before approaching more complex software packages. The goal is to learn as much as possible about both 2-D and 3-D software packages. This will allow you to make more informed decisions when you are working on an actual project.

A Director's Advice: Richard Taylor, Rhythm and Hues

Drawing is something everyone should learn. Learn some of the basic computer tools that are out there, such as Photoshop or QuarkXpress. You can learn them yourself. A lot of people say "well I don't have a computer, and I can't get on one." Well, you can get on one. You have to search out a place where you can get on one, whether it is through your school, library, or a friend that allows you to work on their computer. Wherever you can find a computer that has Photoshop, Quark, Painter, and software programs of this kind. Especially Photoshop, if an individual learns Photoshop they basically learn how to layer images together and some graphics. You need to teach yourself one way or another. There are companies that will teach you what you need to know if you have an art background or if you have a BFA. Some studios are looking for people with an art background to teach them their own software. But generally, you need to know how to use the computer.

If you are going to try to work in a creative field, you need to put a portfolio together that is beyond the student work that you have done. I have looked at portfolios of individuals for years. They show me everything that they have worked on and it is all student projects or some class assignments. I look at that and I say 'Yes that is great but where is your imagination, where is the stuff that you do?' If you are going to be involved in the visual arts field as a creative person then you have to have ideas. If you do not have ideas then you are going to be in the production line part of the deal. You will be an animator or you will do something where you are not picking up the ideas. Not everyone can pick up the ideas. If you are someone with an imagination, you need to put them down in a way that someone can see. Make a short film in black and white; do it in the most inexpensive way that you can. Do some drawings that are your own ideas; do a little film that is a result of your own imagination. If you are looking for creative work, then what your potential employers want to see are your ideas and imagination.

## Internships

Whether you are attending university or college, an institute or being self-taught, if your desire is to work in the industry you should seek an internship. While you are learning, an internship will provide you with real working experience in the field. Look for a company that does what you are interested in doing. So it's best to have an idea of what you would like to specialize in before seeking an internship. Companies are always looking for the best candidate for the job, even when the job is for an intern. Most often the company will ask that you submit a portfolio, resume, and other sketches from a sketchbook to be considered for an intern position at a computer graphics company.

Polar Bear Swim, a 3D computer animation created by Rhythm and Hues

In some of the larger companies such as Industrial Light and Magic, an internship program is already in place for the various specialized areas of production. In smaller firms, such as Curious Picture, the interns might receive more hands-on experience on a project. This is generally true for smaller companies. They hire more in the fashion of master and apprentice. Thus you may have the opportunity to work with the creative director of the company or may even assume the roll of a animator or artist on a project. The smaller the company, the greater the chance to truly work as part of the production team. These types of internships often turn into full-time positions. Historically, companies such as R/Greenberg and Associates usually hire over 75% of their interns to permanent positions.

## On-the-Job Training Methods

Studios are always looking for highly talented individuals that can produce fresh ideas and work well with their team. But a resume and demo reel does not address the issues of how well you work, nor how fast and flexible you are as a prospective employee. Therefore, an internship program can prove to be beneficial to you and also to the studio that is constantly hiring, because internships are used by the studios as a prescreening program for future employment. The studio gets an opportunity to see how well the intern works out, and gets some relatively inexpensive employees in the process. But, the match of intern to studio is mutually beneficial. You as the intern have an opportunity to receive on-the-job training and possibly work on a production. You may also receive more visibility that can lead to a permanent position at the internship location or at another company.

Another form of on-the-job training is the Employees Training Program. This training program is often implemented at larger studios where proprietary software programs are used. This method of training usually takes 6-10 weeks. Its main purpose is to get new employees up to speed and familiar with the company's in-house software. But this training may also be used to train existing employees who may be asked to work on a project that requires the use of an unfamiliar proprietary software. The company's trainer coordinates the training.

### Employee Training Program

On-the-job training is also necessary for entering a company that is using proprietary software. Most companies use a mix of the of-the-shelf software and proprietary software. For those using primarily proprietary software, there is an absolute need for on-the-job training, while others that are using primarily standard commercial software may find that this training program in not necessary. Most companies today require new computer graphic employees to undergo training. This training usually takes 6-10 weeks depending on the company. It is viewed as an orientation to the company and its policies as well as an opportunity for the employees to learn from the practitioners in a hands-on classroom environment.

Xaos, a small animation production company based in San Francisco once operated primarily as a proprietary software based environment. This type of software created a barrier and made it impossible for the new practitioner to learn how to use it before starting work at the company. To overcome this, newcomers were generally taught by senior practitioners and a trainer at the company. Later, the company switched over to a more user-friendly production environment, and now functions as a predominately off-the-shelf software based company.

The company has since documented all its proprietary software and made it available on-line. This method insures that the new employees receive in-depth training on the software. Xaos once used instructional videos and technical directors as a primary method of training. The 24-member company has since formalized their training process and have hired an instructor to assist with education and documentation. However, according to former trainer Roberta Brandao the emphasis on training at Xaos has been hands-on and pragmatic: "mainly, the way you get trained is by doing it and by talking to the people who work with you. That is the way I was trained when I started, and while I was still animating I was already training the new people. As you learn, you already start to teach."

At a larger company such as Pacific Data Images, lead trainer Jennifer Yu acts as more of a supervisor, in an effort to bring together various areas of production. She explains, "involvement is to work with the other animation managers and projection ID (industrial design) people to figure out what everybody should know—what they agree on should be the basis of all the training classes. So it is my job to pick peoples' brains and figure out what the core of the course is. The teachers are all people who are animators or R&D (research and development) people. I sort of oversee the program and track progress. I arrange a lot of the classes for ongoing training as well. I also do documentation and supervise technical writers."

Yu supervises the technical writers to ensure that the hard copy and online help manuals are written with consistency. "So that when people teach," Yu says, "because everyone has a different way of teaching, they all sort of go through the same training points for every class." Yu's outlines provide a model for the delivery of instruction.

The trainers' responsibilities are also to prepare the animators to fulfill the needs of the clients in the most cost-efficient

"The computer might actually be the single common tool that will lead to an integration of various arts, such as music, animation, sculpture, drama, architecture, design and dance."
—A. Michael Noll

way possible and to provide a general understanding of the production company and its functions. This goal is different from that of the universities and other institutions. The theory must be explained to the new employees. The trainers suggest that the ultimate goal of their training programs is to bridge the gap between a formal education and corporate production. As Brandao explains "When you are in a company, there is a much more focused goal. You are producing—that's why it's called production. When you are in a program like Ohio State, the students have their own goals but you are not working in a group environment. There are demands from the teacher, so you are producing, but you are producing for yourself. Another thing that everybody notices is the amount of work that you are expected to produce: the deadlines and the fact that the pressure is tremendously higher when you come to a production company. When you are in an educational program, it is a much more relaxed environment and the focus is not so much to produce as to learn."

At PDI, Yu tries to build on any prior computer knowledge the trainee has obtained from his or her formal education. Those trainees who have traditional film animation backgrounds are acclimated to the computer and its use as a special effects tool. Yu explains that the training program "... assumes that most people will have somewhat of a computer background and have the basics of computer graphics. So as soon as they come in the door we try to give them a really broad overview, not exactly becoming expert on one tool because the class is only about one or two hours a day. But we just give them an overview of what is possible and the way we do things at PDI... There are some people, though, who have never touched a computer before. We had one person coming over who said he'd used a Mac before, but I think he had worked with claymation so it was quite different for him. There are people like that and we need to give them a broader background on how to use the computer."

## Job Training Program Structures
The training structure at production houses usually resembles that of PDI or Xaos. Training is a means of teaching the tools neces-

sary to get the production done efficiently. However, in 1996 a new model of training entered the production world. That is the model established by Pixar. Perhaps one of the fastest growing production companies, Pixar now employs over 400 people. Though they are not all involved directly in production, Pixar has realized the need for continuous education among them, and continues to train its new recruits in the rudiments of production. In 1996, Pixar established Pixar University, a department within the company.

Similar to that of PDI and Xaos, the primary goal of the university is to train new employees on the software used at the company. Pixar, however, has taken its training program to another level. The company assigned a dean to its university, and hires a staff of instructors that teach anything from yoga to animation. Established initially to help train the large number of students that were hired to do production, the university has since begun to address other needs of the company as a whole. "Education is extremely important to Pixar," says Rachel Hannah, then recruiting manager at Pixar. "It was really important for us to get people here and get them going, but now that we have our full production team here it is really critical for us to keep them interested in what they are doing and keep them learning."

The push toward an exemplary level of ongoing internal education is further explained by Randy Nelson, Dean of Pixar University: "We pay a lot of attention to what our members need and what we as a studio need and we attempt to develop that. We have weekly classes which are the primary offering of PU. Our weekly classes span from traditional fine arts through filmmaking and technical skills, animator specific curriculums, items of general interest such as special events, field trips, guest lectures, and master classes. There are eight classes a week offered in the weekly primary curriculum, and each class is two hours long. The term is 12 weeks. A typical offering would be sculpture, introduction to drawing, figure drawing, life drawing, painting, introduction to filmmaking, composition and design, drawing for animators, color, staging and composition, and introduction to editing. The content is heavily weighed toward drawing. The classes are offered to everyone in the studio, so it is not unusual to have an animator sitting next to an accountant, who might be sitting next to a technical director, who might be sitting next to the CTO [Chief Technical Officer] of the company. We have students in every range and at all levels of the company in the classes."

The program at Pixar focuses on education by means of training. Nelson explains the philosophy of the unified goal: "The classes are focused on practical skills because we found that there are several problems that are easily stated but are difficult to solve. Understanding the difficulty of the craft and the difficulty of the person who does the job next to you, not only your job, increases the ability of the people in the studio to communicate. And ultimately, filmmaking is a collaborative art, where the success of the film is a function of how well you are able to articulate a vision. How consistently is that vision translated into the various elements that have to be created by various people, and how that vision comes through from the mind of a single creator all the way to the work of 400 people. Everything we do has at its heart the idea that the degree to which we understand the whole task, and how well we communicate, that is the level at which we will be able to deliver with high fidelity our vision. If you understand what is trying to be accomplished, it is much easier to figure out how you should do that best." As in the case of education programs, the studio's university focuses on mastery of a subject area rather than simply presenting the fundamentals.

The story is at the heart of all production; with this fact in mind, Pixar University has implemented other classes geared toward story development. "We have just finished a year-long effort to focus on developing story skills throughout the studio," Nelson said. "We have done a set of story prerequisite classes in which we had approximately half the studio involved in developing storytelling skills. For example, the ability to tell a story visually, or to act out that story through improvisation, to capture elements through gesture drawing, to render a scene competently through advanced drawing, and following that with outside work and actors. We then went to a Story 101 class that was at the base level taught by an expert at the studio. It focused on basic storyboarding skills including pitching and improving the boards. From there, a small number of people went into a 10-week, full-time session where all they did was work as a production team doing storyboarding and developing skills." During this period, the team also did odd assignments at the studio. This assignment resulted in 10 new full-time story people for the studio.

In part, the ongoing education at Pixar University is fueled by problems brought into the classes by individuals or problems created by the instructor. "It presumes that students bring rich experiences to the class and that they are presented with an opportunity to work on the complex solution that simple problems have," Nelson says. "One of the classes that is a good example is called Composing Pictures, where we look at film composition backwards. We look at great films, break them down, and storyboard them from the film, and then analyze the compositional elements to derive an emotional vocabulary." Such sophisticated problems are resolved through teamwork, and a focus on the individual scenes. "We work in collaboration, and we analyze short sequences of film." The group then shares the results and critiques the storyboards in class. "We attempt to assemble a kind of understanding of the vision that the director, the director of photography, and the creators of a particular live-action film must have had in presenting this. And we discuss how to yield an emotional result from a technique. We do a lot of things where we present simple problems and stand back and let the students work on them."

Educational discussions and mini-conferences help create a third dimension to the education of the practitioners at Pixar. Nelson says: "One of the regular things we do is host a weekly meeting where technical people get together and read graphics journals and choose an article or presentation and just talk about it. We are in the second week of a three-week science fair. Having wrapped the feature, *A Bug's Life*, we got all the various experts and contributors who did all the magic that it took to solve the problems we took on to tell that story, and we are sharing those things in an informal gathering." The graphics journal club and the science fair are only two of the more semiformal gatherings within the company. These gatherings and others allow the company to be a supportive environment for new research, and for the university to be a department in which significant research, no matter how small, is facilitated.

Pixar University grew out of a master apprenticeship model that has always been a part of the studio's history. "There is a strong sense that no matter how long I have been doing this, there is someone in the studio who has been doing this longer than I have," Nelson said. "We are in fact part of a culture that grew slowly and over a longer period of time with individual training and mentorship." In its embryonic stages, the company would hire the best practitioners and team them up with talented senior practitioners at the studio. But the knowledge did not always flow from master to apprentice; it was more of a free exchange of ideas that led to the company's ability to solve complex problems for a job. The high quality of work within the company helps to create a self-motivated environment where practitioners are always reaching beyond the obvious solutions to exceed the expectations of their co-workers and ultimately the audience.

This model of training was created as a more formal program to accommodate a large number of new recruits that were hired between 1996-1998. It was established as a means of preparing the new employees for production during the hiring boom. "We realized that the pool was made up of mainly raw talent coming straight out of school with no industry experience," Hannah says. "So they get here and they would go through an extensive 10-week training class where they would be at Pixar University for 8- to 10- hours a day, learning our software and our style. So they come out of that 10 weeks as prepared for production as possible having no work experience." Hannah clarifies, "It was a matter of looking at the facts, we had a massive hiring, doubling the company, and students now coming out of school."

For the students coming straight out of school and into Pixar's 10-week training program, Nelson said that major adjustments were often necessary for the classes held in technical directing and animation: "Learning to receive criticism on unfinished work is an important thing we find that new hires do not have as a skill from school. They may have understood criticism, they may have understood collaboration, but typically the focus was on getting the thing finished and then doing a critique. In the production environment, at Pixar in particular, we focus on the notion that the best feedback is what you get early on. You want feedback as work is developing so that it can guide you. We spend a lot of time in critique. The work is individual but the results are collaborative; so learning how to integrate your work into a collaborative focus is one of the important elements of these classes. Do not mistake the fact that they are about our toolset, you learn the toolset by way of need. The need is driven by an attempt to achieve style. That is the reason why we focus on internal teaching and mastery of these areas rather than having external trainers or internal trainers who are dedicated just to teaching. We want people to understand what it means to do the work of the studio. That is the heart of these two classes."

Nelson speculates that, "if we were not offering the 10-week session, we would probably still use the materials and do it as a mentoring experience where new hires would be assigned to a master animator from the studio who would bring them up to speed. Using the tools, the focus would be still to create work that is at the level of Pixar finished goods—so that you could say that is the style, that is the way we tell jokes, that is the rhythm. Our beats have a real strong focus on expression even though what you are busy doing is trying to figure out how the tools work."

Traditionally, Pixar's training is grouped into two main categories: Technical Directing and Animation. Trainees are trained to specialize in an area of production. While the normal structure at other companies was more toward a general overview, at Pixar, if you were recruited to be a modeler you were going to be trained mainly on how to use the company's modeling programs. This was the norm at Pixar in 1994. The company trained its practitioners in one area, for example, in animation or digital lighting. Its training sessions were of no specific length, but instead were geared to the needs of each individual trainee. For example, when in 1994, Sharon Calahan, now lighting supervisor at Pixar, transferred to the company after working at PDI. Pixar did not require

Calahan to go through much of a training program. Calahan explains, "they pretty much gave me two days of training and then gave me a packet of shots to start lighting. So I pretty much hit the ground running." Within her two days of training, she met with an experienced practitioner for two to three hours at a time. "They would show me what I needed to know to do a particular task; mostly it was just kind of playing with it until I was comfortable. It was similar enough to other tools I had used, it was primarily a matter of adjusting to a new syntax. The concepts are the same. Experienced TD's (technical directors) can usually make the adjustment to a new set of tools very quickly."

At Xaos, a company that went out of business in December 2001, the training structure was different to that of Pixar. Sessions, related to a specific software package, were generally held everyday for the first two to three weeks. The tightly scheduled classes left little room for further explanations. Former trainer Roberta Brandao explains that "we work on something, and then afterward we go over the basics so the person understands what is going on. If they want to go over it any further and enhance it or do anything extra, then they are encouraged to do that on their own time." Alexei Tylevich, a trainee at Xaos in 1994 recalls, that he generally trained with Brandao for "set hours, generally two days, four hours a day." During his training period, Tylevich was not committed to any mayor project, but instead did parts of different things, according to his ability at the time. He supplemented his "live" training with videotaped instructional documentation produced by the programmer who created the software. After he was trained, Tylevich was assigned to specific projects. He has since worked as an animator on numerous projects at the company.

At PDI, trainees are given four- to six-weeks of training from the day they are hired. Within the training period, they are given "a complete cycle from 2-D all the way to 3-D and lighting." Trainees are assigned 2-D and 3-D projects outside the classroom during the training period. These assignments give the trainee the opportunity to work out the problems they may have before they are assigned to productions. According to Yu, 2-D practice jobs utilize images that are in production already. For the 3-D project, the trainees do "what is called a mock job, where they come up with a small little piece themselves. They storyboard it out and have a producer tell them set schedules, when parts of the project should be completed." With these projects, animators in training get their first opportunities to work on creative projects using the company's available tools. Yu noted, "Some mock jobs actually become personal projects at PDI. Like *Gas Planet;* I believe that one started as a mock job as well."

After they have completed the training program, trainees at PDI are assigned to mentors. Yu explains that "it is difficult to just be thrown in the system. The mentoring process gives the trainee some feedback as well as general support, technical support." Mentors, managers, and even fellow trainees help to evaluate each trainee's mastery of material. As Yu remarks, "If someone wanted to learn a specific technique for a mock job, he or she can work with other people in the group—then those people will give feedback later on. They may say that I helped this person on their mock job and therefore can vow that he or she really knows it well, or that he or she didn't understand some part of it and, if so, the manager will stop by and see how the person is doing. Plus, we ask the trainee a lot of questions."

At Xaos, there were no officially assigned mentors to aid the trainees beyond the educational program. Instead, according to Brandao, a technical director steps in to aid the animators. This particular technical director is not assigned to any specific job. Instead, "he or she works on every job and helps set up things for the animator." This technical director may also assist the animators to develop problem-solving techniques for project efficiency.

Sometimes, trainees are put into production early in the process, before training is completed. Brandao explains, "If there is a production crunch, some people might get pulled off earlier or be asked to work part-time while they are training." In any case, trainees are not tested for mastery before they are placed on production jobs. Brandao explains, "I don't test them. They are tested when they start working on a job. I teach them and it is up to them to tell me if they have understood it or not... sometimes what happens is they don't feel quite confident, or they didn't quite understand something, so we go over it again."

To ensure that new trainees at Xaos keep current with changes in the software after the training, employees are encouraged to become beta testers. New practitioners are able to test the tools being developed by Research and Development personnel, "so from the very start their feedback is incorporated. They are sort of tied to this tool from the beginning." Perhaps the biggest reward for the testers is the feeling that they are not limited by software that already has been developed; rather, their feedback can be incorporated into new design.

At PDI, senior animators attend informal training sessions to keep abreast of changes in software. Sometimes, they will develop procedural pages to share their findings with other animators. Michael Collery, former animation resource director, finds that software is becoming increasingly easy to use, but recognizes that "you can run into trouble when you are dealing with a client or somebody who wants something that the package just can't deliver. But I think if you know what your limitations are, then you start figuring out ways of dealing with the limitations."

Training is a major issue in the field of computer graphics. Although university programs can be useful in providing fundamental knowledge of underlying principles, the variety of software programs being developed by individual companies often makes retraining an essential element of every new position. Software not only varies from company to company, but also from one moment to the next, as producers struggle to stay one step ahead of the competition.

"We are all pursuing much of the same things," Nelson says. "I think that every education program is in some way doing what Disney did, or not doing what Disney did. In the deepest sense, if you are serious about working in an animation house, regardless of whether you use multiplane cameras, stop action or computer graphics, the fundamentals are the same. You are trying to convey a motion, create an impression in your audience, or to create something that is memorable in the heart not in the head. The technology in particular can be a crutch or an impediment when attempting to achieve those goals, because you can fool yourself into thinking that merely delivering something that is visually interesting is sufficient. Obviously, that is not going to last."

### Training at Industrial Light and Magic

So far, we have examined the training structure at large studios such as Pixar and PDI. These companies have several goals in common. They are exclusively involved in the creation of computer-generated graphics, they create animation feature films and visual effects for clients, and their training occurs within a assigned time period. But at Industrial Light and Magic where production is only done for an external client, and often involves a mix of traditional and computer generated effects, the training is often production specific and the period for training varies. "The eye is always toward whatever it will take to create what we need, at the quality we need for a given production. It is always production driven," says Endla Burrow, the training manager at ILM.

"The duration of training," she says "depends on the experience, what they are going to be doing on the project, how long they are going to be on the project, and what their background is. It could be anywhere from as little as a week of time in the training area to several months. With the caveat that the people who are here for a week may be working on a shot that may be mentioned by more senior people." Burrow continues: "It really depends on production needs. For example, if we are working on something where somebody's initial project is desperate for someone to do the really basic task, and they have experience so that I have somebody who comes in and they are a modeler who has worked for years on vendor [of-the-shelf] modeling software, and we need immediately for a particular show to come up with some models. They do not necessarily need to know all of the ILM proprietary software. It is going to take extra weeks for them to get on that show right away. That does not mean that they are fully trained. At a later point, either in their course of working on other shows or in-between shows they would catch up, basically they would learn the other tools."

ILM trains with the understanding that each new employee will be at a different skill level. It is therefore rare that a group of employees are trained together. "Though they may attend some sessions, there is a lot of individualized attention. For example, you would have animators coming in who are completely computer savvy and you have traditional animators who have not done any thing but cell animation beginning on the same day. Totally different fields that need to be focused on. Some of the classes they would share at the same time," Burrow remarks.

Like other large studios, the training continues beyond the entry level. "Ongoing training happens constantly. There are classes that happen formally and informally during the course of shows, because software and technique develop continually so that there will be hours throughout the week where people are meeting in varying sizes of groups for a class and then they will be actually going out and teaching other individuals at their stations. Additionally, if we are making a large scale software change we will have a series of classes where people come down into the training area and have lectures followed up by hands-on practice for several days at a time to get the main gist of how to work around whatever the current software would be. Additionally, we have other classes that are ongoing classes that happen generally in the evenings; we have life drawing, sculpture, animation, and film classes."

### Wei-Chung Chang: From Pupil to Pixar, A Career Path

Chang began an academic career in computer graphics in 1987 at The National Taiwan Academy of Arts now known as The National Taiwan College of Arts in the Department of Industrial Art. At the college, he also received a general design education, studying areas such as Product, Interior, and graphic Design. Chang began to appreciate the computer after learning a 2-D paint program. Still focused on the goal of being an Industrial Designer in 1993, Chang immigrated to the USA in pursuit of this goal. He matriculated into the Industrial Design program at the Ohio State University where be began to study animation using the Commodore Amiga 2000, and its 2-D software Deluxe Paint. After a year at OSU, Chang transferred to Pratt where he worked on the Apple Macintosh. His education at Pratt included 2-D Computer Graphics, Multimedia, and basic 3-D Animation. He completed his BFA at Pratt in computer graphics. After seeing the work of students from William Paterson University at a SIGGRAPH screening, he decided to move to New Jersey to attend the University. There, Chang was introduced to the SGI platform and began creating animated stories. While pursuing his Masters, Chang attended the DECATA Animation Festival at the University. As his animation professor and festival director, I introduced him to Sharon Calahan, a lighting practitioner at Pixar and a participant at the festival, and arranged for her to review his work. Calahan was pleased with his animation and recommended him to Pixar. After receiving a Master of Arts degree in Computer Art and Animation from William Paterson University, Chang went to work at Pixar Animation Studios as a Technical Director in the area of Lighting. A family emergency caused Chang to leave Pixar and assume responsibilities in Taiwan. Chang is now a computer graphics professor at a fine arts college in Taiwan.

Selecting a School

Today, there is an abundance of colleges, universities, and institutes that offer courses and degree programs in computer graphics. When selecting a school, first ask yourself some key questions. What are some of the best methods for preparing for the field I am interested in? What degrees are necessary to enter my field of interest? Am I going to be in proximity to computer graphics companies that offer internships? Does the school have the right mix of art, science, and technology in the curriculum to suit my needs? Should I attend a college, university, or short-term training institute? Which school should I attend? You must also examine yourself, your desires, goals, and your tolerance. There are several ways of becoming educated or trained in any given area in the computer graphics field. The choice of whether to attend a four-year college or university, or whether to attend an institute is often hinged on patience. Four-year universities provide a more in-depth study of the field. The computer graphics curriculum at the university contains a mix of theory and practice; so, the curriculum is geared toward a broader approach to the field. Students at the university are usually required to complete a general education curriculum before entering into their major area of emphasis. This process is often completed in two years for a full-time student. The third and fourth years are usually spent on the major area of emphasis. The goal at the university is to prepare the student for the career through an in-depth approach to the intellectual issues of the field. The university environment and the short-term training programs both have benefits.

## Benefits of the University Education

- Students are awarded a degree, such as a BA or BFA, at completion; this becomes the foundation for advanced studies at the graduate level.
- At the undergraduate level, it is a four year in-depth program.
- More hands-on practice time on the computer after class.
- Greater opportunity for significant feedback from the faculty.
- A mix of practical and theoretical courses.
- Reasonable tuition and in the case of state universities, state residents receive reduced tuition.
- Courses are usually content based, not software driven.
- A nurturing environment for an individual starting an academic career.

## Benefits of the Training Program

- Shorter, more intense, narrowly focused courses.
- Courses emphasize the needs of the industry.
- More practical hands-on courses.
- Often an environment of working professionals that presents networking opportunities.
- Class schedules are usually arranged to suit the needs of working professionals.

As outlined above, the real difference between the university's curriculum and short-term institutions is that of education versus training. Perhaps one of the most important issues for a student entering an academic computer graphics program is this issue. Before researching an academic program, the student should realize that this distinction is made in most academic programs. For example, a student who has graduated from a four-year college may go back to school to be trained on the latest computer graphics tools. On the other hand, a recent high school graduate may seek an education in the discipline. Training is more direct and focused. The trained student will be able to operate a specific software, hardware, etc.; however, the trained individual often needs to be retrained as the software or hardware is upgraded. In the computer art discipline, a trained individual may understand the computer rather than the art and aesthetics; they are technically proficient. An education at a university is more general, not specific to any one hardware or software, but often more theoretical.

When selecting a school, examine the academic curriculum for computer graphics. Computer graphics programs are usually comprised of art, science, and technology. Know which one you are most passionate about and consider selecting a school whose curriculum gives your area priority over the others. If you enjoy art for example, consider a school that has a strong focus in art. If the schools offer excellent programs in art, begin to examine the schools more closely, and ask yourself: What medium do I enjoy working in best? Identify the medium that you enjoy working in and match that desire with the school's offerings in the medium or related materials. It is important to be objective. Consider a school that facilitates a traditional medium you already enjoy working in, and also be sure that they have a strong computer graphics program that facilitates the transition of traditional art forms to digital art. For example, if you enjoy painting, find a school that has an excellent painting area, but that is also teaching digital painting. This will allow you to continue to grow in the traditional medium of your choice while becoming acclimated with computer graphics.

As a student, you must approach education with an open mind. A good solid understanding of aesthetics is still the key to finding employment as a computer graphics artist. While learning different traditional fine arts mediums and techniques, try your hand at computer programming and understanding the computer architecture. Before selecting a school, look at the current demands of the computer graphics industry. Research the trends of the industry. Are they looking for animators today, then what type of skills did they look for five years ago and what do you think they will be looking for four years from now? The answer I am sure will still be someone who can draw well and who understands the aesthetics of the art. Nevertheless, call around to the local animation studios, arrange a phone conversation with a practitioner, find creative ways to meet and talk to people who are doing what you would like to do and get a better feel for the computer graphic industry. Some of the more popular ways to get in touch with professionals are by volunteering at trade conferences and festivals. School field trips to a studio or an invited guest speaker can create and environment for speaking with a professional.

If you aim to work at Pixar as a character animator for the next *A Bug's Life,* you may not wish to pursue a computer science degree. But rather you might wish to enroll in a fine arts school in order to concentrate on developing your observational skills with life drawing, painting, and sculpting, and to learn the basics of filmmaking, character development, and storytelling, while simultaneously learning the craft of cel animation and even claymation. Learning to draw is a skill that requires years of experience. It is not acquired overnight by taking one or two semesters of basic drawing. The development of a unique style demands an investment and commitment all its own. Rachel Hannah, Recruiting Manager at Pixar recommends that students interested in animation "get classically trained, learn how to draw, learn how to act, learn how to tell stories, and make that a priority over learning how to use a computer." A further mastery is demanded to conform a drawing style to the "look" of an animation production. Drawing teaches important and basic lessons in how to observe not only line, form, proportion, texture, color, light and shade, and elements of composition, but also behavior. Observable mannerisms, facial expressions, personality quirks, stance, carriage, and bearing form the building blocks from which a skilled animator depicts a believable character that can breathe life into a story. Similar knowledge can also be acquired and developed by working with other media such as painting, watercolor, sculpture, printmaking, photography, videography, or even from experience with architecture or industrial design.

Technically-oriented students should select a school with a science program that has a computer graphics area of concentration. Hannah advises: "Go to a good school that gives you a focus in computer graphics. The TDs (Technical Directors) here do lighting, shading, or modeling and there are schools out there that focus on these."

If you are interested in graphic design, learn about the current trends in the industry. Join the local users groups and attend conferences, and most importantly keep an eye out for good graphic design when you read a magazine or newspaper. Build your visual literacy. The field of graphic design goes far beyond the knowledge of graphic-design tools such as QuarkXPress, Adobe Illustrator, Photoshop, and Corel Draw. Examining the current trends of most designers show that they are moving toward Web design or digital broadcast video design. The World Wide Web is perhaps the most recent example of how a new technology "retools" preexisting skills and aesthetic practice from previously separate domains. Like desktop publishing or CD-ROM-based multimedia production, successful Web-page development may involve the traditional skills of a writer, art director, graphic designer, typographer, illustrator, painter, photographer, and composer, in combination with the newer expertise of the 2-D & 3-D animator, digital non-linear video editor, software programmer, sound effects designer, cognitive psychologist, and human factors engineer.

When selecting a school, get information on the school's history and some of its successful graduates from the computer graphics area. Request a catalogue from the school that shows the work of the students. If you are interested in animation, call the department and ask for a sample reel of its students work in animation. Speak with faculty in the computer graphics area about the areas of emphasis offered at the school. Speak with some of the current students and graduates of the program. The program director is often delighted to talk about the great programs offered at the school, but do not take his or her word for it—do your own research. What are some of the strengths and weaknesses of the department you are interested in? Some strengths may be the availability of technological tools and small classrooms provides more one-on-one teacher-student relationship. Some common weaknesses of graphics schools today are the lack of qualified faculty and limited access to the technology as a result of short lab hours. Make a checklist of questions. Spend the time and do some in-depth research on the school, which includes its mission and goals. After you have done your research and you are sure of the schools you would like to attend, make a list. Select five schools that interest you, rate them, prepare your portfolio, and begin the application process.

At most schools, whether a training institute or university, there is an open house, or portfolio day. This is an opportunity for you to tour their facilities, meet with the faculty and even with other students. Take advantage of this. Attend several open houses for the schools that interest you. Take notes; later this will help you to make an informed decision if you are indecisive after visiting several schools. Remember that you are interviewing the school as much as they are interviewing you. Continue rating the schools. What is the teacher to student ratio? Are the computer labs modern? Are you comfortable in the environment? Is there enough open lab time and computers? If you are a returning student or one with outside obligations, here are some additional questions you should consider. Are the courses offered at the times that match your schedule? Are the labs and studios open late and on weekends?

Select a training or university program that emphasizes the importance of a high-level of professionalism and problem solving, and the importance of group work as well as the individual as artist. Successful employees need to be able to solve problems and think in terms of broad, underlying principles—and, of course, to be self-motivated in order to learn quickly within the parameters of what may be a brief or even nonexistent training session. Rather than focus on learning one program in detail, it is best for students to strive for breadth by experimenting with a number of software packages. Likewise, in one's education, courses such as the history and aesthetics of film, television, and other arts are necessary for providing a "language" common to people coming to visual effects from many different disciplines.

### Getting In: The Portfolio

At most colleges the admission requirements for undergraduate students include: an application, along with a statement of intent, SAT scores, transcripts, and a portfolio. The art portfolio is a packaged presentation of artwork that best represents you. Find out what is required for your level of admissions, order the application, school catalog, and pay close attention to the deadlines and due dates. Find out if an in-person meeting is required. Even if this interview is not required, make it a point to try and schedule an appointment with the head of the department's committee, or with a faculty coordinator for the area of computer graphics.

The college's art department is chiefly concerned with the quality of the portfolio, and for most schools this is the single most important admission requirement. Therefore, it is important that you pay close attention to the preparation of your portfolio. If you are not able to meet with a faculty member in the department, call and establish contact with the faculty or counselor in order to find out what should be included in your portfolio presentation, beyond the basics: painting, drawing, photography, collage, etc. Are they interested in seeing computer-generated imagery, or such things as short films or videos? As a general note, schools are simply interested in seeing samples or slides of your best work, and only your best work. Show works that you believe are your best and most recent. Do not show a retrospective of your art from years ago. If you are interested in animation, showing additional work reveals your interest in storytelling. Though most schools do not expect that you would have done animation if you are coming directly from high school, such materials as a script, short story, flipbook, or storyboard can help to convey your serious passion and commitment for that area. Presentation completes the package. Your work must be presented in a manner that conveys a high level of professionalism. Mount storyboards, matte printed images, and label all slides.

# Chapter 7
# The Job Market

This is a booming field for both artists and scientists. Companies such as Pixar have grown from 175 people to over 400 in a two-year period. Though the company predominately hires animators and technical directors, numerous positions are available to individuals interested in commercial production. Pixar's leap to doubling its size came from a mass hiring from the school circuit and its quest to find skilled students in the area. Rachel Hannah, recruiting manager at Pixar recalls: "Initially when we were hiring 100-150 people, it was a time when we had to hire a lot of school talent, now the market has shifted and it's the other way around, now there are fewer positions and many more people who want to get into studios."

The process at the time of mass hiring was extremely formalized and prospective employees at Pixar had to be approved at several levels before they could be employed. Hannah explains, "First, we looked at the reel and determined if was a pass or no-pass and then it went to the next step." Hannah then met once a week with a panel of technical directors or senior animators to discuss the reels. If the group accepted the reel, the prospective employee was then invited to an interview at the company. This four-hour interview allowed the candidate to meet with recruiting, then with a hiring manager of the department that was looking, and finally with the group senior animators and technical directors. At this group interview, other supporting portfolio materials are reviewed. "During the group interview, it is a chance for the senior panel to ask questions, and it is also a chance for the interviewee to ask questions," Hannah says. "And within a week we make a decision as to whether we want to present an offer to the person or not." A verbal agreement is then made with the prospective employee, and a one page offer letter is sent to the individual.

At Industrial Light and Magic, practitioners are hired for two major production groups within the computer graphics department—the 3-D group and the digital post-production group. Also referred to as the department's 2-D group, the digital post-production group is made up of rotoscope artists, match movers, compositors, digital matte artists, and 3-D texture painters also referred to as view painters. The 3-D group consists of modelers, envelopers (or model manipulators), character animators, technical animators, and technical directors (or shot coordinators). Within these groups, there are several subgroups, but like most other companies, the two major positions are the character animator and the technical director. Beth Sasseen, recruiting manager for the computer graphics at ILM, explains, that these departments are definitive for the purpose of hiring and placing individuals according to their strengths. "We have very much a skill specific creative group," Sasseen said. "People can have opportunities to cross over once they have been hired."

Animation companies are looking for traditional forms of art in the portfolio of the prospective animation employee. Hannah outlines the qualifications for animators at Pixar: "Good acting, good timing, storytelling is first, and acting ability; we look for people that are trained in hand-drawn classical animation. The computer experience is not necessary at all. In fact, we hired quite a few stop-motion animators, and we have hired two puppeteers from England that turned out to be great, so we take people from all sorts of animation backgrounds but they must be able to tell a story and act. I prefer to see a simple hand-drawn pencil test over any kind of computer animation that people struggle to make pretty. The story has to be clear." John Hughes of Rhythm and Hues agrees and adds, "The specialists that do animation for us are character animators; they are the classical character animators. We don't care at all that they ever see a computer in their life. We care about whether or not they are good animators." These companies may also choose computer animators whose demonstration reels are very simple but incorporate the principles of traditional animation. "There are computer show reels that are very simple figures and objects there are not fully rendered; they show movement and acting," Hannah said.

"The character animators and the technical directors are the easiest fits," Sasseen adds. For every company, the character animator must be able to give life to a form. However, for ILM, a company whose major interest is visual effects for films, other criteria are necessary. "For the sake of ILM, we are replicating something that is life like, integrating something into an live action plate. So the closer a character animator can come to showing us that they can illustrate a sense of believability in stance, in weight, in follow through and all the elements of character animation, the closer they are to being able to animate what we will need them to do." Sasseen continues, "We have movies that have stylized animation in them but even with them it is not the kind of made up animation that an all CG environment will allow you to get away with. There has to be some believability to the character and how they move and how they react and how they interact to make it work for us." In addition, the company looks for some of the common ingredients in a portfolio of a prospective character animator including life drawings, flip book, pencil test, and other examples of their ability to animate.

Artists applying to the 2-D group at ILM may start at the entry level of rotoscoping and advance to creating composites or 3-D texture paintings. In preparing for these positions, the artist should consider showing the building of a short on their demo reel. "They should include the kinds of things where you see how they interpret the information as it is composited together." The process is as important as the final composite. She recommends that prospective employees show the components, and a progressive layering of all elements that make up the final image. The same should be included in the reel of a technical director.

As a visual effects, gaming, and commercial environment, Rhythm and Hues, like most other studios, hires for the areas of animation, modeling, and lighting. According to Hughes, lighting is often overlooked in the university curriculum, though most major studios hire three lighting specialists for every animator and modeler. It requires a lot of different skills to be a computer graphics artist. "At Rhythm and Hues, we typically hire out of Masters degree programs, because it requires maturity and it requires a sophisticated skill set. They need to be sophisticated both technically and aesthetically. They don't need a lot of technology, if they are good at high school level mathematics that is plenty of technology." Hughes continues, "What we really look for is that unique combination of art and technology, coupled with someone that has good moral and ethical sense, and is a self-starter, a good communicator, and a good collaborator." These skills are necessary to work in the teamwork and self-motivated environment.

With an objective to produce an animation feature film yearly, Pixar's 400 plus employees is ample. The company has created two production teams that will ultimately lead to producing one feature film every year. "We are still hiring," says Hannah "we are very selective now." The company will select individuals with several years of industry experience with exemplary talent or exceptional students with desirable skills. This selective screening is prevalent in most of the major animation companies. The qualifications for art-based positions at the studios cannot be generalized; however, most studios are basically seeking a good communicator that is willing to be a team player. Individuals must understand the traditional arts, and knowledge of UNIX and computer programs is a plus.

If employed at a smaller company, you can take advantage of the opportunity to work in different areas of production and learn different things. This can make you a more valuable asset to a larger company. According to Sasseen, the employee of a smaller company needs to "understand the ups and downs and the ebbs and flows and the problem solving that comes from working in a smaller environment. Being solution-oriented when you have no resources or a deadline that is unbelievable. That's exciting," Sasseen said. A position at a smaller company can help to lay the groundwork for this to take place; however, if your intention is to work at a large studio on feature films work hard towards it and you will eventually get there, but do cherish the experiences gained along the way.

## PDI: Selecting and Working with Art Employees

It is no surprise that every computer graphics company is seeking the best employees. The best for an art position in this field often means one who possesses a concrete understanding of the art, and also the role science plays in the production process. Though the standards today have improved to an incredible level of quality in computer graphics productions, it is important to note that companies are still seeking technique more than technology. It is therefore important that you illustrate the stages of production and planning rather than simply showing the polished results produced by the computer. The studios want to see how you move from the concept to the storyboard to the actual finished project, but equally important you must show how the technique serves as a means to creating an impression. "It does not matter if you are a technical director or an animator, ultimately your work is to create an impression, an emotional response in an audience," Nelson says. "We are not looking so much for finish, we know we can teach finish, we've got the hardware, we have got the expertise to be able to get something to looking polished, but give us something worth polishing."

Marilyn Friedman, Director of Recruitment at Pacific Data Images recommends that prospective animation employees prepare a demonstration reel. "The reel should be no more than three- to four-minutes long, with the most favorable work first. If someone has done a film or has another type of project that they want us to view, it is okay to put that at the back end of the reel, and in the cover letter say 'for additional materials please note that I have attached my...' If we are interested we will go to that, but we will be judging 3-4 minutes of the person's best work." In addition, Friedman advises that the prospective employees of collaborative projects include an annotated description of the work identifying the parts they personally created. Include a simple resume. The contents of the resume should include information on software proficiency, education, related work experience, and involvement in extra curricular activities such as SIGGRAPH. "If someone has artwork that supports their reel that is something we do recommend that they send it," Freeman said.

Studios often will not return the demo reels and artwork of the prospective employees, therefore you should always keep the originals and if necessary, original materials should be reserved for in-person interviews. Before PDI created *Antz*, the company's first feature film, they received 300-400 employment applications each month; this number has grown as a result of the movie's success.

At PDI, like at Pixar, the emphasis is on traditional skills with knowledge of the computer application. A sculptor can be attractive to a company like PDI. "Depending on what type of sculpture they do, if it is organic versus geometric or if it is more figurative," Friedman said, "A sculptor transitions well into modeling so that will be a path for somebody." But she admitted that the company is less interested in a person who possesses only the traditional modeling skills. "In the old days, we would bring in a traditional artist and train them on the computer, to get them up to speed on our software. Fortunately, now there are so many people who know how to model in 3-D we don't have to go that way." But all hope is not lost for the traditional sculptor who seeks to work in a commercial studio. "We do sculpture a lot of the characters in small maquette, those are then inputted into the computer, so there are needs for people who can sculpt." Maquettes are commonly used in the various industrial studios were previsualization of the character or product is necessary. This function is often used in commercials, live action, and industrial design projects. Often individuals are hired on a part-time temporary basis to create maquettes. "There are needs as a studio but the person will have to land themselves some place where they've got multiple projects." This will ensure them a full-time job.

It is common for small studios and even larger studios to value the multi-talented employee; however, one should have a major area of specialty. Character animator is probably the most specialized area in the industry, therefore it is rare that they may be transferred to another area or even asked to perform a different task within the studio. But this is not the case for a technical director at most studios. Because technical directors pick up the company's proprietary software quickly, they are likely to be put to the challenge of learning another proprietary tool for another project. "A lot of our CG modelers went on do lighting for *Antz*," Friedman said, "a character animator wouldn't do that. But it just depends on what someone is good at. So we did use people cross-functionally that way. In our commercials and live-action film effects, we actually look for people who can do a broader range of things so that we can staff them in different ways."

The company is shifting toward more specialization of its employees. "People are starting to specialize in lighting, modeling, effects, and character animation. In the old days, people could really do all of that." Today, however the productions are much larger at PDI and it is difficult and costly to staff the production with generalists. "We really look for people who are really good in one or two things. Someone who is visual, we can use them, too. If someone knows that they have an interest in lighting, they should build their education around the fact that they want to be a lighting specialist." Generally, the company is interested in individuals who understand how their area of specialty works within the production process.

Traditional fine arts painters are often prime candidates for the industry. "Digital matte painting is a great area for a fine artist to go," Friedman said. "You really need to know how to paint to be able to do matte painting. That is the requirement, not that you know Photoshop. The requirement is that you need to now everything about fine arts painting." However, employers do require that the artist have an aptitude to work on the computer. But not just any fine arts painter will do. "It will have to be realistic painting. We will have to see that the person could paint a landscape or paint a still life realistically. Our projects are either photo real or stylized real." Therefore, the personal portfolio should emphasize more realistic and less abstract painting as it can be difficult to know if an abstract painter can transfer to a digital matte painter. Slides are used to pre-screen a candidate for a matte painting position at PDI, after which the candidate is expected to present samples of original fine arts images. Similarly, students interested in lighting should understand traditional lighting. This knowledge must be reflected in their portfolio.

Studios often use part-time and temporary employees to handle the short-term jobs. At PDI, this is often the case in their art department. The art department usually employs trained individuals such as set designers and character designers to design for a specific job, and the individual is employed the duration of time the services are needed for a specific task. Because of the commitment necessary to train animators, modelers, lighting specialists, and technical directors on the studio's proprietary software, it is not cost effective for the studio to hire these individuals on a part-time basis.

Immediately after the six-week training, the employees are staffed on production. However, it may take 3 months to a year before they come up to speed. Individuals at PDI are tracked throughout their career at the company and the most senior person may have to learn the newest tools that are developed. "I think that's why people come here," Friedman said "they have the opportunity for constant growth and continued education." Constant training also helps to expand the company's ability to take on new assignments. "Right now we are trying to bring a couple of huge things in the door, and we are stretching for certain kinds of talent because we don't have enough of the people that we need to do these kinds of projects. If we stop developing people, we are never going to have the personnel resources to continue to take on the projects that we are looking for. Once somebody is here and the aptitude is there and they know how to work in this environment we really try hard to make them more robust, so that they can take on more. If they have leadership skills, that's great. If they can lead technical teams that's great. It's a bird in the hand." Throughout the 10-hour average workday, the company has been able to promote a healthy environment with a high retention of its employees. For the production of *Antz*, the company hired over 150 new employees with great success in the area of retention.

Production experience is key. Freeman explains, "We value education, but we do value production experience. And if a student had an internship at a production house, that goes a long way. Coming to work at this kind of facility is very different to being in school, and so if someone can get that kind of experience elsewhere then we don't have to teach them how to work in a production environment." The prospective employees applying for their first job at a studio are not evaluated at the same level with the practitioners at other companies who are seeking to transfer to PDI. Though production experience is not mandatory, it is preferred. "We have hired people who have had no production experience," Friedman said. "For example, we have hired software engineers who did not want to write code any more, but they are very interested in production and filmmaking. So we have taken a lot of very technical people for technical rolls in production."

Stefen Fangmeier, Visual Effects Supervisor, ILM

Stefen Fangmeier's interest in visual effects came by way of his interest in computer science. "Computer science I looked at as something that will have a future and would lead to a future career," Fangmeier said in a discussion of his journey into the field of visual effects. "I actually like logic very much so that got me into computers." Fangmeier began studies in computer science with an interest in software programming. While studying computer science, he realized that images were most interesting part of what appealed to him. "I was working my way through school. I was doing programming, and slowly began to use some computer graphics applications. I did some scientific work for the National Science Foundation, visualizing scientific data. So I started dealing with visual problems, visual communications."

In mid-1980, on a digital production project for Volkswagen, Fangmeier had the opportunity to tackle the issue of visual art on a commercial spot. "They were taking a CAD database of car bodies, and having us do renderings of that. My first major realization that I was becoming a visual artist was the fact that I was looking at this car, which was on a turntable that we were rendering. I was looking at the bumpers and saying, 'Now what do bumpers look like?'" This sparked an internal discussion for Fangmeier who had no formal art education, as to how one represents an object realistically within the computer medium. "On my way to and from work I was looking at car bumpers," Fangmeier said. "I realized that the way to gain the visual art of computer graphics, you really need to become a visual analyst studying everything around you visually looking at it and really seeing it and taking it in." He continues, "In computer science you have an analytical mind to solve these problems, I sort of took that skill that I developed there and I applied it to the visual aspect, going to the museums and looking at paintings." This has also helped Fangmeier in simulating the aesthetics concerns of reality in his role as a visual effects supervisor.

In his job as visual effects supervisor, Fangmeier works directly with the client, often the film director and the production team. Throughout the production process, he is responsible for maintaining a relationship with the client on behalf of the studio. This may include reviewing shots and making suggestions to the director on the movie set to working at the studio in the post-production stages to motivating and directing the artists. In fact, his role on a project is similar to that of the director except that he is limited to the visual effects portion of the film. "When I get on to a project, I am sort of the lead person here at the company working directly with the director and providing these visual effects," Fangmeier said.

"At the beginning of a project when they have gotten the script, we usually bid the work. We read through the script and we provide a solution for what they want to do. I do that together with a producer. So I look at the ways of creatively and technically solving the problem and then the producer figures out how much it will cost. Then we provide that as a bid. When we actually get awarded the work, I will work with the production team, that is the production designer, producer, director of photography, the director, set designer, and pre-production getting ready to the point where they will start filming the movie. I then go on set for all the scenes that will have our work involved. I will be present working with the director on the shot as it is being filmed. It is very important for me to give input or to be there and observe that so that we can later on take that scene and put our work into it and be most effective. Then once that film gets here, it is scanned in and then our artists work on it, and I will on a day-to-day basis supervise that work. On most projects, it is a group of 70–80 individuals."

Fangmeier did not always have this amount of responsibility when he first began at ILM in 1990 as computer graphics shot supervisor for *Terminator 2: Judgment Day*. From this early stage, he began working with mentor Dennis Muren, one of the studio's chief visual effects supervisors. On the film, Fangmeier was responsible for supervising the computer graphics for one scene within the movie, rather than that for the entire movie. Then, his duty included working directly with the computer graphics artists and programmers to create the computer-generated imagery for the scene. He then moved to computer graphics supervisor in 1991 on the movie *Hook*, then to lead computer graphics supervisor in 1993 on the blockbuster hit Jurassic Park, and finally to digital character co-supervisor in 1995 on *Casper* with Dennis Muren. He has been a visual effects supervisor since being given the title in 1996 for the movie *Twister*.

His journey from CG shot supervisor to visual effects supervisor allowed him to explore and appreciate the various areas of specialization. The key to working as a supervisor Fangmeier said, "Is a combination of technical skills, of just knowing the tools that you are working with, the creative skills of being a visually strong person, and on top of that, being a good people person." Fangmeier continues, "People management skills, motivation abilities, leadership qualities, and some sort of production smarts to know ultimately what is good enough. The one thing that I really learned as an artist from Dennis Muren is how to know when something is good enough to be in the movie. Especially in the digital effects medium, you can change every aspect of it and you can fiddle things to death. But if you then see it in the movies and it plays through once, you say 'that really wasn't worth it.'"

Understanding how the various areas come together is

an important skill for the visual effects supervisor. "We have people with various skills here," Fangmeier said. "We have visual effects supervisors who don't have a computer graphics background, who used to do optical work or miniature work, like Dennis Muren, who get educated in digital tools. Since you have CG supervisors who can answer all those questions, so you don't have to be that technical. I find that knowing the underside of it, knowing the innards of the machine that I am using, the tool and how the tools are actually built and what they are actually doing helps me understand. If you are a racecar driver, just knowing what exactly goes on in the engine. You don't really need to know how an engine works necessarily or the details of it to be a good race car driver, if you just know how to drive well. But if you do know that, I think it helps you even more. So it is not necessary but by knowing that I know what the tools can do and I can direct the person that I am supervising more effectively. Knowing, for instance, how hard it is to do what you are asking for."

Though it is not necessary for the visual effects supervisors at ILM to be technically proficient in the details of the software programs at the studio, Fangmeier finds that knowing the programs can help to expedite the production. "I am still sitting at the keyboard trying to keep up with that [computer software]," Fangmeier said. "Sometimes the easiest way to communicate something, sometimes is to sit down and do a little example on the computer. It is difficult to keep that skill up and not lose it, but to me I still enjoy it." The responsibilities of being a supervisor does not allow Fangmeier to sit for long hours at the computer keys himself, instead, he must use his day for several different individual and group meetings with the various production team members. "You really are a slave to the production. My day-to-day routine as far as how much time I actually have to myself is fairly limited because all the time people need to get input from me."

Overall production is much like farming, Fangmeier explains, and the role of the visual effects supervisor is much like a farmer. "You plant your seed, that's when we do a bid, and some design. They go on location and shoot the film, then you watch it grow. Then the harvest comes in, that is the film gets here and we do the work. In the winter, the film get released and you do all of the publicity. Then the next project starts. As a visual effects supervisor you are affected by this cycle. After completing the project, there is often a period of down time while waiting for the next project, while CG people will move onto other projects more readily."

Fangmeier's success can be attributed to his willingness to go beyond his formal education of computer science to studying art and film aesthetics. Fangmeier's position allows him to work directly with lead directors such as Steven Spielberg and various members of the production team. This provides him with an opportunity for practical hands-on learning. Once a student who moved from music because of a fear of the theoretical aspect dominating the study, Fangmeier's present position is a happy medium. "I didn't want to go for a Masters," he recalls, "I was more into doing and applying my skills." Learning everything he knows about film directing on the job, Fangmeier hopes to one day direct computer animation feature films. He is a true testament to the success of on-the-job training. "I never had any idea that I would end up working on Hollywood films, and now I have progressed to the point were I am planning to direct computer generated films." He continues, "Every two or three years I discover 'Oh wow, I am really interested in that' and I could have never predicted that." This sense of changing discoveries, Fangmeier said is the result of analyzing and learning from the environment at ILM.

## Self-Employment

There are several options for the self-employed computer artist. The two main forms of self-employment are through freelance and small business ownership. Whether directing a project as a freelance director or working on an individual project, the self-employed computer graphics artist is often working in a group environment. Most self-employed artists may find that some important assets include the ability to direct individuals on a project.

Proper communication skills, then, are crucial for the self-employed artist. Other requirements for becoming a successful self-employed artist are supervisory, management, and administrative skills.

Often, small studios depend on freelance practitioners to work on production, and more new corporations are choosing to form alliances with other companies rather than hire permanent employees. To keep the daily expenses at a minimum, the company must bid and receive a project before hiring freelance workers. Small studios often function as a sort of animation showroom for larger companies, or to show what can be produced in alliance with a larger studio. They may bid and receive large jobs only to farm them out to other companies, smaller or larger studios. They may also depend on subcontractors to do all of the work. This can cause problems of coordination among companies, as the small company often relies on outside freelancers of large companies to assist as subcontractors. "When you are bidding against other companies like Rhythm and Hues, Digital Domain, or ILM," Richard Taylor, a former small studio partner explains, "you actually have to subcontract them, so you can't mark that up; it's all past due money." He adds, "I didn't necessarily have access to the people I wanted and needed to use all the time. If they were booked on a project at the time." At the company, Taylor was often hired by the major studios to direct commercials or he hired the studios to work on a contract he had won. Operating without any equipment, he relied on the availability of studios to create the animation.

With the price of computing equipment at an all time low, computers are more accessible than ever before. For a person interested in self-employment as a computer artist, there has never been a more suitable time to enter the field than now. The first step in becoming self-employed is to determine exactly what your goals are. Do you want to create high-end animation like in the style of *Toy Story*, or are you more interested in designing products, or creating fine arts for gallery exhibitions? With that information in mind, begin to outline a business plan. There are several books on business plans that you can refer to at your local library or bookstore. This is important, as it is the first step to drafting and thinking of the mission, objective, and market for your work. Next, determine exactly what equipment is needed and whether it is best to purchase, rent, or lease it. You may also want to consider buying used equipment. Other considerations include workspace; consider working out of your home to keep your start-up costs low. Before you purchase that computer, do some market research to determine who are your clients and to better understand your market.

## Final Thoughts

Perhaps there is some truth to the old saying, "What is old is new again." As we look at the development, as we look at design in general, whether clothing or product, it seems like our future has been predetermined by our past. A good case is the design of the Apple computer and its retro look, or the fact that a girlfriend recently showed up to a date wearing bell-bottom style jeans of the 1960s. I couldn't help but think if I had only kept my clothes from the 60s...oh well, they wouldn't have fit me anyway. But what does this all mean for the creative mind, the artist, the animator. It simply means that understanding the past can give you a keen insight into the future of computer animation. Little is invented, a lot is innovated.

We have made major progress in the development of the tools for computer graphics and animation. We have successfully compacted the computers. Now, a computer takes up less space than an artist easle. Today, the flat screen monitor continues that trend, no more traditional CRT displays, now we are free to use the computer table for a lot more planning space. Space on which better storyboards can be drawn; thus, creating more clever animation. I urge you to use this desk space wisely. Computers are cheaper. What cost millions 30 years ago can now be purchased for pennies on the dollar. New, affordable computers have made the field more accessible to all, and that is great news. Not to mention the fact that most computer buyers are over sold by the clever salesperson who encourages you to buy 100 megs when you may only need 20. So cheaper can mean cheap tricks to get more from the consumers. But computers are not only cheaper today, they are faster. They are able to process higher quality graphics in a fraction of the time it took larger computers to process half the quality decades ago.

A trend has been set by cel animation studios to go overseas; we wait to see if 3-D computer animation will follow. Realizing that it is cheaper to create an animation overseas, cel animation producers started the trend of farming out the grunt work to other countries, thus slowing the growth of national studios. This is unfortunate but not unusual for industries in America. We create it, sell it, patent it, and then send it out to be developed elsewhere. If this is true then we must become "chiefs" (i.e. artists who understand the administration aspects of the field). Learn more about producing and directing and being on the administration team of an animation project, or becoming the next Bill Plympton, a one-man animation studio. All is not lost, as with 3-D computer animation. In the stop-motion arena, most of the popular series seen on TV are still done nationally. But it is increasingly difficult to tell which ones are being done overseas. There is no required label as in the case of the clothing industry that reads "Made in America." The 3-D computer animation studios such as Pixar and PDI/DreamWorks have started the trend of creating 3-D computer animation features, but the jury is still out on whether further 3-D films will request assistance overseas.

# References

Abbott, L. B. (1984). *Special effects: Wire, tape, and rubber band style* Hollywood: ASC Press.

Archer, S. (1993). *Willis O'Brien: Special effects genius.* Jefferson, North Carolina: McFarland and Company, Inc.

Artist and Computers. (1967, April). *Ohio State University Monthly* 58, pp. 4-5.

Azarmi, M. (1973). *Optical Effects Cinematography: Its Development, Methods and Techniques.* Unpublished doctoral dissertation, University of Southern California.

Bailey, A. (1982). *Walt Disney's World of Fantasy.* N.Y.: Everest House Publishers.

Barnouw, E. (1981). *The Magician and the Cinema.* N.Y.: Oxford University Press.

Baur, T. (Ed.). (1993). *Special Effects and Stunt Guide.* (1989). Beverly Hills, CA: Lone Eagle.

Blackman, B. (1987). *Special Effects for Print Art Directors, Designers, and Photographers: A Menu of Unretouched Special Effects.* NY: Van Nostrand Reinhold.

Blandy, D. (1983). *Printing Poetry in Blissymbols: An Art-of-the-Boob Apprenticeship for So-called Mentally Retarded Persons.* Columbus, OH.: Ohio State University.

Bloska, A. (Speaker). (1994). *Interview.* (Cassette Recording No. 002c) San Francisco: Gardner, G., Doctoral research.

Bohmer, B. (1988, September 30). OSU Professor Pioneer in Computer Art, Design. *The Ohio State Lantern*, p. 11.

Bonifer, M. (1982). *The Art of Tron.* N.Y.: Little Simon

Boyle, D. (1990 October). Ed Emshwiller, 1925-1990. *Afterimage,* 18, 3, 3.

Brandao, R. (Speaker). (1994). *Interview.* (Cassette Recording No. 002a) San Francisco: Gardner, G., Doctoral research.

Briggs, J. (1988, October 2). Csuri Go To Extremes to Express a Common Artistic Vision. *The Columbus Dispatch*, pp. 1G, 2G.

Brosnan, J. (1974). *Movie Magic: The Story of Special Effects in the Cinema.* N.Y.: St. Martin's Press.

Bulleid, Henry Anthony Vaughan. (1954). *Special Effects in Cinematography.* London, Fountain Press.

Calahan, S. (Speaker). (1994). *Interview.* (Cassette Recording No. 004b) Richmond, CA: Gardner, G., Doctoral research.

Canemaker, J. (1977). *The Animated Raggedy Ann and Andy: An Intimate Look at the Art of Animation, its History, Techniques, and Artists.* Indianapolis, IA: Bobbs- Merrill.

Catmull, E. (1998, July). *Visions. Film & Video.* p. 146

Cawley, J., & Korkis, J. (1990). *How to Create Animation.* Las Vegas, NV: Pioneer Books, Inc. (p. 12).

Csuri, Chuck. Computer World. (date unknown). *Columbus Dispatch* Magazine.

Collery, M. (Speaker). (1994). *Interview.* (Cassette Recording No. 002a) Sunnyvale, CA: Gardner, G., Doctoral research.

Cook, C. J. et al. (1980). *Trickfilm/Chicago '80.* Chicago, IL: School of the Art Institute of Chicago.

Cooper, J. D. (1979). *Special Effects, Shooting Situations and Darkroom Techniques.* Garden City, N.Y.: Amphoto.

Cosner, S. (1985). *Special Effects in the Movies and TV.* N.Y.: Julian Messner.

Culhane, J. (1981). *Special Effects in the Movies: How They Do It.* N.Y.: Ballantine Books.

Csuri, C . (1985, December 5). *Charles Csuri to Present Commencement Address on Campus,* p. 4.

Csuri, C. (Speaker). (1994, 1995). *Interview.* (Cassette Recording No. 001b, 003a) Columbus, OH.: Gardner, G., Doctoral research.

Dale, R. (Ed.). *Education, Training and Employment.* N.Y.: Pergamon Press.

Delaney, B. (1994, August). Virtual Reality Lands the Job. *New Media,* 40-48.

DeMaria, J., D. (1991). *A Study of the Work of Charles Csuri, Computer Artist and Art Educator.* Unpublished doctoral dissertation, New York University, N.Y..

Dickson, W. K. L., & Dickson, A. (1970). *History of the Kinetograph, Kinetoscope and Kinetophonograph.* N.Y.: Arno Press.

Douglas, C. (1994, December), Toon Town. *Wired* 94- 104.

Fielding, R. (1965). *The Technique of Special-Effects Cinematography.* N.Y.: Hasting House.

_____. (1985). *The Technique of Special-Effects Cinematography,* (4th ed.). London and Boston: Focal Press, (pp. 1-10)

Finch, C. (1984). *Special Effects: Creating Movie Magic,* (1st ed.). N.Y.: Abbeville Press.

_____. (1988). *The Art of Walt Disney.* N.Y.: Crown Publisher, Inc.

_____. (1993). *Jim Henson: The Works.* (1st ed.). N.Y.: Random House.

Fleeman, M. Studios Look to Dethrone Disney in Animated Market. *Entertainment Herald & News.* Nov. 21, 1998. p.88.

Fraenkel, J. R., & Norman, W. E. (1993). *How to Design and Evaluate Research in Education.* (2nd ed.). NY: McGraw-Hill, Inc.

*Frames: A Section of Drawings and Statements by Independent American Animators.* (1978). Unpublished, N.Y.

Frierson, M. (1994). *Clay Animation: American Highlights 1908 to the Present.* N.Y.: Twayne Publishers.

Fry, R., & Fourzon P. (1977). *The Saga of Special Effects.* Englewood Cliffs, N.J.: Prentice Hall International, Inc.

Gardner, G. (1997). *Guide to Computer Graphics Animation and Multimedia Schools.* Wayne N.J.: Garth Gardner Co. Publishing.

Gardner, G. (1995). *Informal Computer Art Education.* Unpublished dissertation. Ohio State University.

Gardner, G. (1998 September vol. 8 no. 9). *Procedural Animation: An Old Concept Revisited. Silicon Graphics World,* p. 16.

Gardner, G. (1999 January). Wanted a Few Good Animators. *Computer Graphics World.*

Gates, A. (1984, June 24). ABC Deal Allows Computer-graphics Firm to Build Reputation. *The Columbus Dispatch Business Reporter.*

Gilmer, L. (undated). Morphing to the Madness. *Cinefex,* 52, 88-89.

Glassner, A. (1989). *3-D Computer Graphics: A User's Guide for Artist and Designer.* Second Edition. N.Y.: Design Books.

Goodman, C. (1987). *Digital Visions Computer and Art.* N.Y.: Harry N. Abrams, Inc., Publishers.

Goetz, P. W. (Ed.). (1987). *The New Encyclopedia Britannica* (15th ed., vol. 1). Chicago: University of Chicago.

Goldstein, S. (1993, July 25). The Amazing Colossal Men. *Image,* 14-21.

Halas, J. (1984). *Graphics in Motion: From the Special Effects to Holographic.* N.Y.: Van Nostrand Reinhold Company.

_. (1990). *The Contemporary Animator.* London, England: Focal Press.

Hall, J. (1990, April 29). Csuri Brilliantly Utilizes Computer. *The Columbus Dispatch,* p. 7F.

_. (1991, May 21). Csuri's New Angle. *The Columbus Dispatch*, p. 8F.

Hamilton, S. H. (1990). *Apprenticeship for Adulthood: Preparing Youth for the Future.* N.Y.: The Free Press.

Harryhausen, R. (1981). *Film Fantasy Scrapbook.* (3rd ed.). La Jolla, California: A.S. Barnes and Company, Inc.

Hass, R. (1985). *Special Effects in Photography.* London, England: Dent.

Hayes, R. M. (1986). *Trick Cinematography: The Oscar Special-effects Movies.* Jefferson, N.C.: McFarland & Company, Inc.

Hayward, S. (1984). *Computers for Animation.* London, England: Focal Press.

Head, G. (1975). *Special Effects.* Pittsburgh, PA: University of Pittsburgh Press.

Heraldson, D. (1975). *Creators of Life: A History of Animation.* N.Y.: Drake Publishers.

Hilfinger, H. (1941). *A Study of the Significance and Application of Special-effects to the Cinema.* Unpublished masters thesis, University of Southern California.

Holland, E. (1979, Spring). The Electronic Marvel Invades Man's Creative Domain. *OSU Quest.*

Unknown, *Hollywood Production Digital Style.* (1994, July). *New Media*, 36-42.

Hutchison, D. (1987). *Film Magic: The Art and Science of Special Effects.* N.Y.: Prentice Hall Press.

Imes, J. (1984). *Special Visual Effect: A Guide to Special Effects Cinematography.* N.Y.: Van Nostrand Reinhold Company, Inc.

Jacobs, L., and Roberts, J. (1947, March). Mr. Csuri's Double Life. *BMOC.*

Jaccobson, L. (Ed.). (1992). *CyberArts: Exploring Art and Technology.* San Francisco: Miller Freeman, Inc.

Jaeger, J. (Ed.). (1988). *Complementary Methods for Research in Education.* Washington, D.C.: American Education Research Association, (pp. 277-323).

Kaufman, J. (Speaker). (1995). *Interview.* (Cassette Recording No. 006c) Columbus, OH.: Gardner, G., Doctoral research.

Kerlow, I. V., Rosebush, J. (1986). *Computer Graphic: For Designers and Artists.* N.Y.: Van Nostrand Reinhold.

Kerlow, I. V. (1996). *The Art of 3-D Computer Animation and Imaging.* N.Y.: Van Nostrand Reinhold.
Kinsley, J. L. (1983). *Apprenticeship in Craft: Expanding the Role of the Art Educator.* Unpublished masters thesis, The Ohio State University, Columbus Ohio.

Krug, D. H. (1993). *An Interpretation of the Expressive Cultural Practices of Non academically Art-educated 'makers of art' in Wisconsin.* Unpublished doctoral dissertation, University of Wisconsin, Madison WI.

Kursh, H. (1965). *Apprentice in America: A report on Golden Opportunities in Industry*. N.Y.: W.W. Norton & Company, Inc.

Lafferty, M., B. (1994, March 7). Movies, TV Ads Have OSU touch. *The Columbus Dispatch*, pp. 1C, 2C.

Laurel, B. (Ed.). (1990). *The Art of Human-computer Interface Design*. Reading, Massachusetts: Addison-Wesley.

Leeman, R. W. (1985). *Design and Curriculum considerations for a Computer Graphics Program in the Arts*. Unpublished masters thesis. The Ohio State University, Columbus, Ohio.

Livingston, K. E. (1985). *Special Effects Photography*. N.Y.: Amphoto.

Lobb, C. (1982). *Exploring Apprenticeship Careers*. N.Y.: Richards Rosen Press, Inc.

Lurye, R. (Speaker). (1995). Interview. (Cassette Recording No. 008ab) Columbus, OH: Gardner, G., Doctoral research.

Maanen, J. V. (1988). *Tales of the Field on Writing Ethnography*. Chicago: The University of Chicago Press.

Madsen, R. P. (1990). *Working Cinema: Learning from the Masters*. Belmont, CA: Wadswoth Publishing Company.

Manen, M. V. (1990). *Researching Lived Experience: Human Science for an Action Sensitive Pedagogy*. N.Y.: State University of New York Press.

McCarthy, R. E. (1992). *Special Effects Source Book*. Boston, MA: Focal Press.

McDevitt, M. J. (1986). *Computer Graphics Orientation and Training in a Corporate/Production Environment*. Unpublished masters thesis. Ohio State University.

Merriam, S. B. (1988). *Case Study Research in Education: A Qualitative Approach*. San Francisco: Jossey-Bass Publishers.

Merritt, D. (1987). *Television Graphics-from Pencil to Pixel*. N.Y.: Van Nostrand Reinhold Company.

Miller, P. (July 1998). *Art and Technology*. IEEE Spectrum. pp 19-28.

Mirapaul, M. (October 15, 1998). Retrospective for Pioneers of Computer-based Art. *New York Times* (online).

Morrison, M. (1994). *Becoming a Computer Animator*. Indianapolis, IN: Sams Publishing.

Neale, S. (1985). *Cinema and Technology: Image, Sound, Color*. Bloomington, IN: Indiana University Press.

Negroponte, N. (1994, December), Digital Expression. *Wired*, 222.

Patton, M.Q. (1990). *Qualitative Evaluation and Research Methods*. (2nd ed.). Newbury Park, CA.

Pascall, J. (1977). *The King Kong Story*. London: Phoebus Publishing Company.

Pinchbeck, D. (1994, December), State of the Art. *Wired*. 156-159, 206-208.

PDI Takes the Pillsbury Doughboy into 3-D Animation. (1992, December 18). Back Stage *Shoot*.

Preston, S. (18 April 1965). *The New York Times*. p X23.

Quigley, Jr., M. (1948). *Magic Shadows*. N.Y.: Biblo & Tannen Booksellers and Publishers, Inc.

Quinn, M. (1993). Beyond the Valley of the Morphs. *Wired* Premiere Issue, 57-59 106.

Rheingold, H. (1991). *Virtual Reality* (1st Ed.). N.Y.: Summit Books.

Russett, R, and Starr, S. (1988). *Experimental Animation: Origins of a New Art.* N.Y.: Da Capo Press, Inc.

Saks, R. (Speaker). (1995). *Interview.* (Cassette Recording No. 009ab) Columbus, OH.: Gardner, G., Doctoral research.

Schechter, H., and Everitt, D. (1980). *Film Tricks.* N.Y.: Dial/Delacorte Sales.

Schwartz, L. F. (1992). *The Computer Artist Handbook.* N.Y.: W.W. Norton & Company, Inc.

Shanahan, W., F. (1983). *Guide to Apprenticeship Programs.* N.Y.: Arco Publishing, Inc.

Shapiro, M. (1994, September). Behind the Green Mask, *Comics Scene 46,* 33-37.

Shay, D., and Duncan, J. (1993). *The Making of Jurassic Park.* (1st ed.). N.Y.: Ballantine Books.

Skalsky, C. (1992, October). Pacific Data Images. *Film & Video.* 58-62.

Sklar, R. (1993). *Film: An International History of the Medium.* N.Y.: Harry N. Abrams, Inc.

Slattery, J. (1988, February 8). Computers Serve as Art Medium. *The Ohio State Lantern,* p. 11.

Slayton, J. (Speaker). (1994). *Interview.* (Cassette Recording No. 003a) San Jose, CA: Gardner, G., Doctoral research.

Smith, T. (1986). *Industrial Light and Magic: The Art of Special Effects.* (1st ed.). N.Y.: Ballantine Books.

Solman, G. (1993, July ). Dateline, Prime Time: 500 nations. *Millimeter, the Magazine of Motion Picture and Television Production.* 32-42.

Solmon, L. C., Bisconti, A. S., & Ochsner, N. L. (1977). *College as a Training Ground for Jobs.* N.Y.: Praeger Publishers.

Solomon, C. (1994). *Enchanted Drawings: The History of Animation.* N.Y.: Alfred Knopf.

Soter, T. (1994, January). Brave New World. Special Report: Animation, *Shoot.*

Spellerberg, J. E. (1980). *Technology and the Film Industry: The Adoption of Cinemascope.* Unpublished doctoral dissertation, University of Iowa, Iowa City, Iowa.

Swan, S. D. (Speaker). (1995). *Interview.* (Cassette Recording No. 006a) Columbus, OH: Gardner, G., Doctoral research.

Tart, D. (Speaker). (1994). *Interview.* (Cassette Recording No. 004a) Richmond, CA: Gardner, G., Doctoral research.

Thomas, B. (1991). *Disney's Art of Animation from Mickey Mouse to Beauty and the Beast.* N.Y.: Hyperion.

Thomas, B., and Merritt, D. (1993). *The School-to-work Transition and Youth Apprentice: Lessons from the U.S. Experience.* N.Y.: Manpower Demonstration Research Corporation.

Trachtman, P. (1995, February). Charles Csuri is an 'Old Master' in a New Medium. *Smithsonian.* 56-65.

Tylevich, A. (Speaker). (1994). *Interview.* (Cassette Recording No. 002b) San Francisco: Gardner, G., Doctoral research.

Watt, A. and Watt, M. (1992). *Advanced Animation and Rendering Techniques.* N.Y.: ACM Press

Weinstock, N. (1986). *Computer Animation.* Reading; Addison-Wesley Publishing Company, Inc.

Whitney, M. (August, 1997). The Whitney Archive: A Fulfillment of a Dream. *Animation World Magazine.* (online)

Wilkie, B. (1989). *The Technique of Special Effects in Television,* (2nd ed.). London; Boston: Focal Press.

Wills, C., and Wills, D. (1980). *History of Photography: Techniques and Equipment.* N.Y.: The Hamlyn Publishing Group, Limited.

Yin, R. (1984). *Case Study Research: Design and Methods.* Beverly Hills, CA: Sage Publications, Inc.

Yu, J. (Speaker). (1994). *Interview.* (Cassette Recording No. 005) Sunnyvale, CA: Gardner, G., Doctoral research.

Zippay, L. (Ed.). (1991). *Artists' Video: An International Guide.* N.Y.: Cross River Press.

## Appendix A: Glossary

**Acetate**—Also called a cel when used in traditional animation. A clear sheet of plastic on which the animated characters are inked and painted.

**ACM**—Association of Computing Machinery.

**Algorithm**—Mathematical based programming string or code.

**Analog**—A device that computes actual voltages, or analog signals directly. The analog system can be programmable but the processing would have to be done by adding together voltages and signal levels rather than binary.

**Animation**—Perceived motion caused by the rapid display of a series of consecutive still photographs, drawings, or computer generated stills that differ slightly. On video, these frames are usually played back at 30 frames per second, and in film an average of 24 frames-per-second to create a motion that best simulates real-life movement.

**Animationologist**—One who studies various aspects and forms of animation.

**Anti-Aliasing**—A computer process used for removing jaggies by smoothing the edges of a digital image so that it appears to be more like a photograph.

**ASCII**—American Standard Code for Information Interchange. A standard code that assigns a unique number to each character in the English alphabet along with other special characters.

**Behavioral Animation**—An animation technique that allows each character to use the same motion as the other characters around him while moving in different directions.

**Binary**—Having only two positions, ON and OFF, or 0 and 1. An electrical switch could be considered a binary switch since it is either on or off and there are no other possible settings.

**Bit**—Binary Digit—A binary unit of storage that can represent only one of two values, ON and OFF, or 1 and 0.

**Bump Mapping**—A program or code that can be applied to a 3-D computer object to create a rough or bumpy surface appearance without deforming the actual geometry.

**Byte**—A unit of storage composed of eight bits. One byte can store a numeric value from 0 to 255, or one letter.

**Calibration**—Color correction to adjust the hue, saturation, and value of video.

**Cel**—Short for celluloid, this is a clear acetate that is used in traditional animation. Cels allows the animator to composite layers of images.

**CG**—Computer Graphics. Graphics that are created on the computer or that are scanned into the computer and made digital.

**CGI**—Computer-generated imagery. This term is often used in the motion picture industry to describe computer graphics in films.

**Character Animation**—Animation of an animate or inanimate object to simulate a given character's personality. This was traditionally done using cel animation, and has been adapted by 3-D computer animators. Character animation usually incorporates the Disney principles of animation.

**Cibachrome**—A photographic printing technique.

**Claymation**—Also called clay animation. This form of stop-motion animation uses a series of photographed clay characters to form an animation.

**CMYK**—A four color separation of colors, usually done to prepare an image to be reproduced through a mechanical printing press.

**Color Correction**—The process by which a color is adjusted to enhance or correct the color of an image.

**Compositing**—Layering of two or more images to form one final image. Example: to create a dog running through a forest, the forest can be rendered as a separate image and the running dog as another, the two can then be layered to form one image. This process usually takes place during the rendering and post-production stages of a project.

**CPU**—Central Processing Unit of a computer. The brain of the computing system.

**Cray**—A brand of computer manufactured by Cray Research, Inc. for super computing.

**CRT**—Cathode-ray tube, this is the formal name for a television picture tube.

**Cursor**—An indicator within an open software program that shows the users where the preceding inputted information will appear.

**Data**—All information inputted and stored in a digital computer.

**Digital**—A computer system where numbers are converted to digital information, such as images displayed on the monitor. Programming through binary arithmetic.

**Digitizing**—The process of converting an analog object or information into a digital format.

**Disney Principles of Animation**—12 fundamental principles created by Walt Disney Company that governs the movement and expressions of animated characters in a scene.

**DPI**—Dots Per Inch. A medium for measuring pixels or dots on the computer monitor that controls the quality of the output. The greater the dots per inch, the better the quality of the image.

**FACT**—Fusion of Art and Computer Technology.

**High-end**—Computer workstation that is capable of producing broadcast quality graphics. It is also used to describe a high quality of graphics.

Hue—Color of an image.

**Image-based Modeling**—A 3-D model that uses an image, such as a photograph, as the basis for constructing the geometry. Image-based models are usually constructed from several different photographs of a single object, taken from different angles.

**Image Processing**—The processing and manipulation of an image, often a photograph, within the computer.

Input device—Devices used to get information into the computer. The keyboard and mouse are common examples of input devices.

**Volume-based modeling**—Models that are constructed through parametric representation or polygons. 3-D modeling.

**Image Morphing**—A procedure that transforms a 2-D image into another 2-D image over a number of frames. Morphs can be 2-D or 3-D and vector-based (lines), or raster-based (photographic).

**Jaggies**—A step-like appearance on the edges of a low-resolution image.

**Low-end**—Refers to the quality of the computer and the resulting graphics. A consumer grade of hardware is usually not capable of producing broadcast quality graphics therefore it is referred to as a Low-end computer.

**LPI**—Lines Per Inch is used to describe the resolution of the screen

**NURBS**—Non-Uniform Rational B-Spline, is an algorithm that accurately defines a free-form curve through more simplistic geometry.

**Off-the-shelf**—Usually refers to computer software or hardware that is commercially available.

**Output device**—Devices used to transfer information from the computer to another source. A computer printer is a common of output device.

**Morphing**—Derived from the word Metamorphosis, morphing is used to describe a technique in animation that involves the transformation of one object into another. There are two main forms of morphs volume morphing and image morphing.

**Monochrome**—Of one color, black and white.

**PC**—Personal Computer. First introduced in 1975, the term is used today to identify window-based operating systems.

**Pixel**—A single unit of digital information displayed.

**Pixelation**—A style of traditional animation that uses a progression of still frame live action. The live actor acts as the stop-motion character.

**Procedural Animation**—A means of applying a program or code to an object or surface to animate and control some attribute of the form. This can be done implicitly through programming scripts or explicitly through sliders that control various parameters of the object. Commonly used to animate such 3-D objects as water, clouds, and fire.

**Proprietary**—Software or hardware that is create for in-house use only and is not commercially available. Home-brewed software.

**PDP**—Programmed Data Processor.

**RAM**—Random Access Memory.

**Raster Graphics**—Graphics that are formed through the storage of a group of pixels. This form of graphics display replaced the vector display.

**Render**—A procedure used to produce a finished image with assigned lights, textures, and shaders to a 3-D object. To create the finish of an image, render the image.

**RGB**—Red, Green, and Blue.

**ROM**—Read Only Memory.

**Scaninate**—An animation system is a video synthesizer capable of producing real-time animation. Unlike stop-motion film animation, real-time video animation uses computers to completely calculate, update, and electronically manipulate the artwork during the actual taping process.

**Shaders**–A texture that is created through the use of a program in a 3-D computer environment. Shaders can vary from simple color variation to complex ramps used to create wood grains. Shaders are also called procedural textures as they are generated by through an algorithm.

**Shareware**–Software that is created and made available to the general public on a trial basis, with the agreement that if the user becomes interested in the software a registration fee will be paid to the author.

**SIGGRAPH**–Special Interest Group In Computer Graphics. A yearly summer conference organized by an ACM of the same name.

**Simulation**–To create similar to, or equal to that of the object in the real world. To simulate an object through modeling or movement through animation.

**Speech Recognition**–A software program that allows a computer to analyze and interpret human voice.

**Spline**–An adjustable mathematical curve within a what that represents a smooth movement or shape of an object.

**Stop-motion**–A series of film photographed images of an object that is moved or manipulated slightly in each single exposure, so that when they are played back, it creates the illusion of continuous motion.

**Storyboard**–A storyboard takes the verbal information of a script and convert it to visual images in a 2" X 3" format.

**Supercomputer**– A large computer system developed with the emphasis on fast processors and high-performance quality.

**Texture Mapping**–The process, within the computer, of applying a 2-D image onto a 3-D object. Several textures can be mapped to a single 3-D object to create a specific surface quality.

**Turn-key**–See Off-the-shelf. Software that is available at the store.

**Vector graphics**–Lines used to define an image on the computer. This was the early form of computer graphics display of the 1950-70s.

**Volume Morphing**–Smooth deformation of one 3-D object into another through procedural animation.

**Z-Buffer**–An area of memory devoted to holding the depth data for every pixel in an image.

**3-D scan**–An input device used for transforming the dimensions of an actual object into 3-D computer geometry. The scanning is usually done via a laser light.

**Appendix B: Periodicals**

**Computer Graphics and Animation Periodicals**

*Advanced Imaging*–Technical issues relating to science and forensics

*Animation Magazine*–Traditional animation, and general issues in animation.

*Animation World Magazine*–Online animation publication.

*CGI Magazine*–Computer graphics and animation magazine.

*Cinefex*–Traditional and digital special effects for feature films.

*Computer Graphics World Magazine*–3-D computer graphics and animation.

*Creative3-D.net* –Online computer animation news and reviews.

*Daily Variety Magazine*–Film magazine, entertainment news.

*Digital Imaging*–Computer graphics in commercial and fine arts.

*DV Magazine*–Digital video magazine.

*Game Developer Magazine*–Gaming design and general computer game issues.

*HOW*–A graphic design creativity, business and technology magazine.

*ID Magazine*–Design magazine, for product and graphics.

*IEEE Computer Graphics and Applications*–Serves users of computer graphics applications in the arts and science.

*Interactively*–Interactive Web TV publication.

*Mac Design Magazine*–Macintosh magazine for artists and designers.

*Millimeter*–Computer-generated imagery and digital special effects.

*On Production*–Digital effects in movies and commercial productions.

*POST*–Hollywood special effects magazine.

*Videomaker*–Consumer approach to video making.

*Visual Magic Magazine*–online publication.

*Wired*–General issues relating to technology and new media.

*3-D Artist Magazine*–Art of 3-D computer animation.

*3-DLinks.com*–Online computer animation news, and product review.

## Appendix C: Brief Biographies of Main Contributing Practitioners

### Endla Burrow
Heads Industrial Light and Magic's in-house training program.

### Sharon Calahan
Lighting supervisor at Pixar Animation Studios. Calahan's film credits include: Director of Photography for Pixar's *Toy Story 2,* Director of Photography for *A Bug's Life*, and Creative Lighting Lead on *Toy Story*. She has worked in the computer animation industry for over eighteen years where she has specialized primarily in lighting. Before working at Pixar, Calahan worked at Pinnacle Production and Pacific Data Images.

### Wei-Chung Chang
Chang began an academic career in Computer Graphics in 1987 at The National Taiwan College of Arts in the Department of Industrial Art. In 1993 Chang immigrated to the USA. He majored in Industrial Design program at the Ohio State University and recieved a BFA at Pratt in Computer Graphics. He earned a Masters of Art degree in Computer Art and Animation from William Paterson University. Chang work as a Technical Director at Pixar Animation Studios in California. Chang is currently a computer graphics professor at a fine arts college in Taiwan.

### Michael Collery
Michael Collery is currently a Technical Supervisor at PDI/DreamWorks. His most recent film credit is as Matte Painting Technical Supervisor on the feature animation, *Shrek*. With over 20 years of professional animation experience, before joining PDI, Collery was Director of Animation at Cranston/Csuri Productions, a pioneer computer animation studio that was cofounded in 1982. He is a gradutate of the Ohio State University

### Charles A. Csuri
Charles A. Csuri is an artist, computer graphics pioneer, and former professor at the Ohio State University. He exhibited his paintings in New York City from 1955-1965. In 1964, he experimented with computer graphics technology and in 1965 he began creating computer-animated films. In 1967, the 4th International Experimental Film Festival in Brussels, Belgium awarded him the prize for animation. His work was highlighted in the exhibition Cybernetic Serendipity held at The Institute for Contemporary Art, London, England, 1968. One of Charles Csuri's computer films is in the collection of New York's Museum of Modern Art.

**Larry Cuba**

Larry Cuba produced his first computer animation in 1974. A graduate student at the California Institute of the Arts, Cuba solicited access to the mainframe computers at NASA's Jet Propulsion Lab and taught himself computer animation by producing his first film, First Fig. In 1975, John Whitney, Sr. invited Cuba to be the programmer on one of his films. He has been an active participant in animation, film, and computer graphics festivals.

**Stefen Fangmeier**

Stefen Fangmeier is currently a visual effects supervisor at ILM. Stefen Fangmeier joined the computer graphics department at Industrial Light and Magic in 1990. His first major project was *Terminator 2: Judgment Day*. Since then, he has worked on various projects including *Hook* and *Jurassic Park*, as a computer graphics supervisor, *Casper* as the digital character co-supervisor, *A Perfect Storm* as visual effects supervisor, and many others. In 1997, Fangmeier won a British Academy Award for work as visual effects supervisor on *Twister*. Fangmeier received his degree in computer science from California State University of Dominguez Hills in 1983.

**Marilyn Friedman**

Marilyn Friedman is the Head of Studio Recruitment and Staffing at PDI DreamWorks. First hired as a PDI production manager, Friedman has also held the position of Head of Recruitment. She is a graduate of the University of Colorado, Denver with a Bachelor of Arts in Sociology. Friedman has sat on advisory boards at Cornell, California State University, Hayward, and Bournemouth University. She also frequently speaks at North American and British universities and industry conferences on careers in the animation industry.

**Rachel Hannah**

Ms. Hannah began her career as the Computer Graphics Recruiting Manager at Industrial Light and Magic, a division of Lucas Digital where she staffed the crews for the commercial division, and their films *Dragonheart, Jumanji,* and *Twister.* Hannah then joined Pixar Animation Studios to hire Animators and Technical Directors for Pixar's *A Bug's Life, Geri's Game,* and *Toy Story II.*

**John Hughes**

John Hughes is the president and cofounder of Rhythm and Hues Studios. Prior to founding Rhythm and Hues, John worked at Robert Abel & Associates where he participated in the development of motion control camera systems. In addition, he was a technical director on many award-winning commercials. Hughes graduated from the

University of Minnesota where he received his B.A. in Economics and an M.S. degree in Electrical Engineering.

## Keith Hunter

Keith Hunter heads the Model Department at Rhythm & Hues Studios. Keith holds a Bachelor's Degree in Architecture from the Ohio State University and a Masters Degree in Architecture from Harvard University. During his six years at the studio, he has supervised the model work on *Spawn, Batman & Robin, Speed II, Kazaam, Waterworld, Hocus Pocus, Star Trek, The Experience*, and the Academy Award winning feature for best visual effects, *Babe*. In addition, Kevin helped create the models for the famous Coca Cola Polar Bear commercials and the award-winning Sea Creatures in Seafari, an MCA theme park ride film in Japan.

## Ken Knowlton

Ken Knowlton is a computer graphics-pioneering scientist and artist who currently works with mosaics, particularly those made of seashells. He works at NetWaveInc.com, developing techniques for easy and safe use of Internet browsing for children and for adults, plus e-commerce. Knowlton earned a Ph.D. at M.I.T. in 1962. He later worked at Bell Labs for 20 years. In addition, Knowlton worked 5 years at SRI+DEC+misc in CA, 8 years at Wang, 2 years as a consultant, 3 years at NetWaveInc.com, and 2 years as an ACM speaker. He has written many papers on Computer Graphics, and holds 20 US patents.

## Billy Klüver

In 1966, Billy Klüver cofounded Experiments in Art and Technology (E.A.T.), a not-for-profit service organization for artist and engineers, and has served as the president since 1968. Billy Klüver was born in Monaco in 1927, and grew up in Sweden. He earned a Ph.D. in Electrical Engineering from the University of California, Berkeley in 1957, where he served as a professor from 1957-58. For the next 10 years, he was a member of the technical staff at Bell Labs, and holds 10 US patents. He has curated or been curatorial advisor for fourteen major museum exhibitions in the United States and Europe. He has published numerous articles and has collaborated with artists such as Jean Tinguely, Robert Rauschenberg, John Cage, and Andy Warhol to create art that incorporates new technology. In 1998, he received an honorary doctorate in fine arts from Parsons School of Design.

## Carl Machover

Carl Machover is president of MAC, a computer graphics consultancy. He is also an Adjunct Professor at RPI, president of ASCI, past-president of NCGA, SID, and Computer Graphics Pioneers, on the editorial boards of many industry publications, and writes and lectures worldwide on all aspects of computer graphics. He was the History chair for SIGGRAPH '98, and co-executive producer for the SIGGRAPH movie, "The Story of Computer Graphics."

### Mark Malmberg

Mark Malmberg is the Creative Director at Radium, and a former Creative Director of Xaos, Inc., where he worked since 1988 till the company closed in 2001. Malmberg spearheaded the company's creative design and computer animation efforts. These have included works for MTV's *Liquid Television*, for which he won a prime time Emmy Award, the opening I.D. for the "Sci-Fi Channel," and he was selected as one of seven top designers in the country to animate the NBC Peacock ID. He also designed an entirely computer-generated music video for *The Grateful Dead*, and special effects for feature films such as *The Lawnmower Man* and *The Pagemaster*. Prior to joining Xaos, Malmberg worked as a sculptor and musician after receiving an MFA degree in sculpture and painting from the University of Berkeley and a BFA degree at Carnegie Mellon University.

### Manfred Mohr

Manfred Mohr is a fine artist and pioneer of computer graphics. Born in 1938 in Germany, he studied art in Pforzheim, Germany and Paris, France. A self-taught computer scientist, Mohr made his first computer drawings in 1969. Mohr lives and works as independent artist in NYC and is a member of the American Abstract Artists. He has received several awards for his automated drawings including an Artists' Fellowship from the New York Foundation for the Arts 1997, Prix Ars Electronica 'Golden Nica', Linz Austria 1990, and the Camille Graeser Award, Zürich Switzerland 1990. Mohr has exhibited his drawings frequently and has held exhibitions in Germany, Switzerland, France, Belgium, Canada, and nationally.

### Randy Nelson

Randy Nelson is Dean of Pixar University; he began his computer career as a teacher of software development at junior college in the 1970s. After graduation in fine arts from the University of Santa Clara, Randy worked as a Systems Analyst in an IBM mainframe shop. He later cofounded the Flying Karamazov Brothers. At FKB, Randy worked as writer, director, performer, graphics designer, and bus driver. Randy left the FKB to join NeXT Computer, Inc. to establish and lead NeXT's developer training, going from object manipulation on the stage to object manipulation in the classroom. Randy comes to Pixar from Kaleida Labs, where he ran education, and Apple Computer, where he was Senior Curriculum Designer.

## A. Michael Noll

A. Michael Noll is a computer graphics pioneer. He is currently a professor at the Annenberg School for Communication at University of Southern California. Before joining the Annenberg School in 1984, Professor Noll had a varied career in basic research, telecommunication marketing, and science policy, both at AT&T and Bell Labs. He spent nearly fifteen years performing basic research at Bell Labs in Murray Hill, New Jersey. He is one of the earliest pioneers in the use of digital computers in the visual arts, in force-feedback systems, and in raster-scan displays. In the early-1970s, Professor Noll was on the staff of the President's Science Advisor at the White House.

## Ron Saks

Ron Saks is a Professor of Media Studies, at Columbus College of Art and Design where he teaches courses in time-based media design, animation, computer animation, film, and computer graphics. Saks has over 20 years of experience in animation, special-effects animation, and computer animation for film and television. In addition to producing his own independent projects, he has worked on major theatrical releases such as *Time After Time, Star Trek: The Movie*, and *Resurrection*, as well as numerous television programs and commercials. Before coming to CCAD in 1988, he worked for Universal Studios and Cranston-Csuri Productions. He received his BA from UCLA in fine arts and an MFA from UCLA in theatre arts/film animation.

## Beth Sasseen

Beth Sasseen is the Recruiting Manager at Industrial Light and Magic.

## Lillian Schwartz

Lillian F. Schwartz is a pioneer in computer graphics. Her work is represented in major art collections and museums around the world, and as been exhibited at the Museums of Modern Art, the Whitney Museum, the Moderna Museet in Stockholm, the Georges Pompidou, Centre Beauborg, and Grand Palais museum in Paris. A frequent lecturer at universities throughout North America, she has been a visiting or adjunct professor at Kean College, the University of Maryland, New York University, and the School of Visual Arts. For many years, she has been a consultant in computer graphics at AT&T and Bell Labs.

## Alvy Ray Smith

Dr. Alvy Ray Smith, Graphics Fellow, Microsoft: Cofounded four centers of computer graphics excellence before joining Microsoft as first Graphics Fellow: Altamira, Pixar, Lucasfilm, NY Tech. He received a technical Academy Award for alpha channel concept. He received a second technical Academy Award for digital paint systems. Smith invented, directed, originated, or was otherwise instrumental in the following developments: first full-color paint program, HSV color model, alpha channel, Genesis Demo in *Star Trek II: The Wrath of Khan*, first Academy-Award winning computer-generated short *Tin Toy*, first computer-generated film *Toy Story*, Academy-Award winning Disney computer animation production system CAPS, and the Visible Human Project. Smith serves on the Microsoft Art Committee.

### Richard Winn Taylor II
Currently a director at Rhythm and Hues, Richard Taylor has an extensive background in live-action direction, production design, special effects, and computer-generated images for theatrical films and television commercials. In 1971, Taylor received the prestigious Cole Porter Fellowship from USC where he earned an MFA in graphics and photography. In 1973, Taylor helped found Robert Abel and Associates, the pioneer TV commercial graphics/special effects studio, where he served six years as a director. While at Abel's, Taylor created many award-winning commercials, and received four Clio awards. In 1978, Taylor became the first person to computer animate the entire human form with the creation of "Adam Powers" and design and direct effects for *The Looker*. He created special effects and computer generated effects for Walt Disney's *Tron*.

### Jennifer Yu
Jennifer Yu is the director of IT (Information Technology & Training) at Pacific Data Images (PDI). Yu is responsible for the documentation of PDI's animation system and technical training and creative development for the animation staff. Yu is also in charge of PDI's intranet, production tracking system and management of third-party animation software. A graduate of Stanford University with a B.S. in Biology, Yu previously worked for five years at NeXT Computer in Publications as a localization project manager.

# Index